For Hathrel

JUST ACROSS THE FIELDS

FLE

Books should be returned or renewed by the
last date stamped above

Awarded for excellence
to Arts & Libraries

Also available in this series:

Fred Archer	BENEDICT'S POOL
Peter Austen	THE COUNTRY ANTIQUE DEALER
Mary Barnard	THE DIARY OF AN OPTIMIST
Pip Beck	A WAAF IN BOMBER COMMAND
Adrian Bell	THE CHERRY TREE
Mary Sydney Burke	THE SOLDIER'S WIFE
Jennifer Davies	TALES OF THE OLD GYPSIES
Roger Hutchings	CRYSTAL PALACE VISTAS
Ken Hankins	A CHILD OF THE THIRTIES
Herbert C. Harrison	THE MILL HOUSE AND THEREABOUTS
Gregory Holyoake	THE PREFAB KID
Erma Harvey James	WITH MAGIC IN MY EYES
Joy Lakeman	THEM DAYS
Len Langrick	SNOWBALL: GO FIND YOURSELF A SCHOOL
Florence Mary McDowell	OTHER DAYS AROUND ME
Madeline MacDonald	THE LAST YEAR OF THE GANG
Angela Mack	DANCING ON THE WAVES
Brian P. Martin	TALES FROM THE COUNTRY PUB
Roger Mason	GRANNY'S VILLAGE
Cicely Mayhew	BEADS ON A STRING
Christian Miller	A CHILDHOOD IN SCOTLAND
Katharine Moore	QUEEN VICTORIA IS VERY ILL
J. C. Morten and Sheila Morten	I REMAIN, YOUR SON JACK
Pauline Neville	PEGGY
Humphrey Phelps	JUST ACROSS THE FIELDS
Angela Raby	THE FORGOTTEN SERVICE
Phyl Surman	PRIDE OF THE MORNING
Doreen Louie West	LOUIE: AN OXFORD LADY
Elizabeth West	HOVEL IN THE HILLS
Hazel Wheeler	HALF A POUND OF TUPPENNY RICE
William Woodrow	ANOTHER TIME, ANOTHER PLACE

JUST ACROSS THE FIELDS

Humphrey Phelps

ISIS
LARGE PRINT
Oxford and Orlando

First published in Great Britain 1976
by Michael Joseph Ltd.

Published in Large Print 2001 by ISIS Publishing Ltd,
7 Centremead, Osney Mead, Oxford OX2 0ES, and
ISIS Publishing, PO Box 195758,
Winter Springs, Florida 32719-5758, USA
by arrangement with Humphrey Phelps

British Library Cataloguing in Publication Data
Phelps, Humphrey
   Just across the fields. – Large print ed. – (Reminiscance series)
   1. Phelps, Humphrey 2. Country life – England –
   Gloucestershire (England) – Social life and customs
   I. Title
   942.4'1'084'092

ISBN 0-7531-9637-9 (hb)
ISBN 0-7531-9640-9 (pb)

Printed and bound by Antony Rowe, Chippenham and Reading

"The smiles, the tears,
Of boyhood's years,
The words of love then spoken;
The eyes that shone,
Now dimm'd and gone,
The cheerful hearts now broken."

Thomas Moore

CHAPTER
ONE

"To reap and to sow . . ."

By 1942 I'd quite made up my mind to become a farmer. I was eager to leave the grammar school I attended in the market town and begin my education by going to work on a farm. My father, who had a hardware shop in the village, was non-committal. My mother wanted me to remain at school, pass examinations and in due course work in a bank — her sister was married to a bank manager.

Uncle George, my father's brother, was firmly against schools, examinations and banks. Uncle George was a small-holder and a bachelor; and, according to Mother, who had pretensions to gentility, uncouth. Much to her annoyance I spent a lot of time on his holding, and he, to her further annoyance, was a frequent visitor to our home. He came to dinner every Sunday — that is, to our mid-day meal.

After dinner, Father and Uncle would sit facing each other in easy chairs in front of the fire, and discuss the topics of the week: principally local gossip and the scandals in that day's *News of the World*. Oh yes — and I almost forgot — doctors. Uncle considered himself an authority on doctors. He knew which doctors were "first class", and those who were "no bottle". He knew which doctors at the hospital were "coming men" and those who would "soon be in Harley Street". Uncle also spoke at great lengths about his ailments and the miraculous remedies he'd found to "counteract them".

"Here," he'd say, fishing with a thumb and forefinger into a waistcoat pocket, and producing an advertisement cut from a newspaper, "look at this, capital stuff, see they speak very highly of it. Look, here it is, in black and white. What can't speak can't lie. Just the stuff for my trouble, I'll warrant."

There they'd sit, talking for hours on end. Two middle-aged men: Uncle stout and several years the senior, and Father, small and wiry. Their very seriousness, the long pauses and the weighty way they delivered their pronouncements, their sage looks and the solemn way in which they nodded their heads, the puzzled, exaggerated expressions of surprise or disgust, gave the whole performance a comical air.

Father and Uncle also talked about farming. Nearly every man in the village, whatever his calling, had an intimate knowledge of farming. Our countryside was one of small farms; of orchards, woodlands, and streams bordered by alder and willow trees. Oak, ash, and tall elm trees grew in the hedgerows and the soil was rich and heavy. Until the advent of war almost all of the fields were in grass. The farmers kept dairy cows, beef cattle and sheep, and perhaps pigs and poultry — though it was usually the farmer's wife who kept the poultry. Then when the war started the imported cattle food became scarce and most of the pigs and poultry had to be slaughtered. The County War Agricultural Executive Committee — commonly called the War Ag — came into being to supervise the ploughing-up campaign. Some farmers grumbled about being forced to plough; they grumbled even more about having to grow potatoes. They grumbled about the shortage of concentrates for their animals, but most of all they grumbled about some of the War Ag officials who came round to inspect their farms. They resented men who had themselves been unsuccessful at farming now telling them how to farm.

Our farming reverted to an older system; farms now had to become self-supporting and to produce as much food for humans as possible. In many cases the old skills of ploughing, growing corn and roots, and harvesting had to be relearned. And side by side with this came many innovations, the greatest of them being the tractor. Few could have realised what a revolution it would bring to farming.

We had all sorts of farmers, good and bad. It was the latter, the muddle men, who grumbled most. Somehow or other, whatever its shortcomings, the War Ag had to try to make these men produce the maximum amount of food. If all else failed the War Ag could take possession of the farm and in some cases they did, although it was said by many that the farms the War Ag ran were some of the most inefficient.

"I hear the War Ag's been after Burgum again," said Father, one Sunday afternoon.

"So I suppose," replied Uncle George. "I do hear tell he's bin told to get his place together or they'll have him out.

"I'll warrant they had none too good a reception," replied Father. "They got my sympathy, he's a foul-mouthed varmint."

Uncle George wrinkled his nose and pulled a face like one might make after taking something sharp and sour. "I don't mind a bit of honest cussing," he said, "but Burgum do turn out some nasty, filthy stuff."

"I don't hold with that kind of talk, George."

"Oh," said Mother, who'd just come into the room, "that cratur!"

"Ah, he's a bad bagger and no mistake," said Father with an air of finality.

"He's a bad 'un where women's concerned," said Uncle George, who liked to lace his conversation with scandal and if possible some slanderous reference to Mrs Peabody, who was Mother's great friend. "They do say no woman's safe where he's concerned. Young 'uns or old 'uns be all the same to him."

"Oh, the wretch!" exclaimed Mother.

"They do say 'im's got kids all over the place, and that he's got three sisters over at Twistleton in the fambly way," said Uncle George.

"I never heard the like on't," said Father.

"Nor I never have," said Uncle George.

"There ought to be a law against such goings on," Mother muttered.

"No law 'ud stop it," Uncle George said, and puffed out his cheeks. "No law nor nothing can stop 'em when things are like that. They're about, these randy 'uns, as we all do know, but 'pon my soul, Burgum's the wustest I ever heard of in all me born days."

"It's his wife I feel sorry for, breaking the poor little wench's heart," said Father, shaking his head and noisily sucking in his breath.

"The poor thing," said Mother "I don't know whatever she saw in the cratur."

"No more do I," agreed Uncle George. "He could never 'ave bin nice, not even as a babby."

"He's a damn bad bagger and no mistake. There seems to be a devil of a lot of bad baggers got about nowadays. I don't know what it's all coming to." Father screwed up his face and sucked in his breath again.

"He should be horsewhipped," said Mother, and sniffed.

"I do hear tell," rumbled Uncle George, looking very solemn and rubbing the side of his nose with a forefinger, "that he've got some fancy 'oman a-living up there with him, besides his wife."

Father jerked his head up. "Have he, begod!"

"Fouling his marriage bed I call it," sniffed Mother. "I can't stop here and hear any more of it. It makes me go hot all over. I don't know what Mrs Peabody will say when I tell her."

"Her might be glad of 'im," said Uncle George. "Old Peabody can't be much good to 'er, seeing as 'im's allus got 'is guts full o' beer."

"I won't stop here another minute," shouted Mother, and out she flounced, flinging her right leg and slamming the door behind her.

"You shouldn't have said that, George," reproved Father.

"I didn't mean any harm."

"Ah, but Ethel don't see it that way, George."

Father turned to me and said, "Here, go and tell your Mother your Uncle's sorry for what he said. And then ask her to make us a nice cup of tea."

I went into the kitchen and gave Mother the message. She returned with me to the living-room. She planted her arms akimbo, causing Father to remark, "When a woman stands like that, she intends to have a barney and no mistake."

Mother stared down at the two brothers and they looked up at her, stupidly owlish, with rounded eyes. "Now look here, you two, I'm telling you once and for all, I've got something better to do than work my fingers to the bone lushing you up, you great idle men, with cups of tea."

"Now then, Ethel, don't be like that," pleaded Father.

"Hu, hu, hu, hu," grunted Uncle George, in his silly, comic serious manner.

"You squat there, the two of you, and expect me to wait on you hand, foot and finger, while you go on with your disgusting talk," Mother replied.

"Make us a cup of tea, Ethel, my dear," pleaded Father.

"Tea's rationed and so's sugar."

"I'll let you have a pound of my bee sugar," promised Uncle George.

"There, there," said Father in soothing tones, "our George have promised you some sugar."

"Huh, a sprat to catch a mackerel," Mother snorted.

"You make a lovely cup of tea. Bring us a few of they Welsh cakes, or them other little 'uns you was a making, old lady. By gum, them cakes of yourn do knock them boughten things into a cocked hat," said Father.

"None of your soft soap, and not so much of your 'old lady' either."

"Ethel, my dear, you're one of the best. Ain't that right, George?"

"You never spoke a truer word. Ethel's a capital cook, absolutely first class," replied Uncle George.

"Oh yes," said Mother, "you can both be as nice as pie when it's something for your great stomachs." She left the room, but I could tell from her face that she was mollified. She didn't slam the door this time either.

Uncle George belched. "That reminds me," he said, fishing in a waistcoat pocket, "I'd better take another charcoal tablet." He produced a small, flat, oblong tin, opened it and took out a black tablet, which he popped into his mouth. "Capital things, these tablets," he told us as he sucked.

Father seemed lost in thought for a while, then suddenly he announced, "Burgum's a bad 'un, George."

"Ah," said Uncle George, stroking his chin. "His place is a shambles. Wild hedges, broken gates, doors off their hinges; his stock half starved, his fields smothered in weeds. Of course he's never there to attend to the place. He wants pulling up or kicking out. But," Uncle George paused a moment, "some o' they on the War Ag bain't no bottle neither. Broken-down farmers who couldn't make a go on't theirselves, telling others how to go on."

The two brothers lapsed into silence, apparently deep in thought.

7

A little later Father held his right hand up, closed an eye and jerked the back of his head towards the kitchen door. "Hark, hark," he said, twisting his lips and opening his mouth wide enough to show some rotten stumps of teeth. "I can hear Ethel rattling the tea-cups, soak me bob if I can't. We shall be all right for a cup of tea now, George. She don't mean one half of what she do say, George, bless 'er 'eart, she don't."

"Burgum's no bottle, no bottle at all. I 'ouldn't buy nurn a beast off him. He'd do you, sooner'n look at you. That reminds me, after we've had a cup of tea, what about taking a stroll over to Cordwell's? He've got a little bunch of teas that'd just suit me, to run in my orchard."

"I don't hold with dealing on a Sunday, George."

"Oh, I wouldn't dream of buying 'em today. I 'ouldn't even make a bid for 'em. But there'd be no harm in just taking a look at 'em."

"Daresay you're right, George. We'll pop over and have a look at 'em directly."

Mr Cordwell had been at Pound Farm for the last eight years. A small, lean man in his early sixties, he had sharp piercing eyes which darted and danced as he spoke. Sooner or later he'd say, "When I was down in Wiltshire," or "When I was down in Hampshire", or if it wasn't Wiltshire it would be "down in Dorset", or Cornwall, or Somerset. He must have farmed at some time or other in most of the south-western region of England. Occasionally, he would name a district instead of a county, such as, "When I was down in Berkeley."

The slightest thing would set him off on a long rambling tale beginning with, "When I was down —", Though liked well enough — it would have been difficult to dislike a man who was obviously so friendly — he was regarded as not much of a farmer, being inclined to fuss and fiddle. "No idea how to get about a job," was Uncle George's verdict.

He was helped by his two sons, one about eighteen, the other a year or two older. They were happy-go-lucky young men. Mr Cordwell would often grumble about them, but in an affectionate way. "They won't get up in the mornings. We'd get on a sight better if they did. Up all night and abed all morning, that's their trouble. Apart from that they're good boys."

Though Mr Cordwell may have been ineffectual with his own farming, he was always ready with a fund of advice for others. Advice which he'd gathered from experiences down in Hampshire, or Cornwall, Wiltshire, Dorset or Somerset. I saw quite a lot of him, because he was frequently in Father's shop buying nails and staples and, when he could get it, barbed wire. I'm sure he used as much of these commodities as almost all the rest of Father's customers put together. The shortage of barbed wire was a constant source of irritation to him. Barbed wire could only be obtained now by producing a permit from the War Ag.

"I can't understand their mentality," he'd say, pacing up and down the shop. "Barbed wire is a priority, you can't farm without it. Good fences make good animals, good animals make good neighbours. They should have practical men on these War Ags, not these damned theorists."

His animals, it was said, got out and strayed more than any other farmer's. And he couldn't really put it down to the barbed wire shortage. Before the shortage he'd been heard to say, "When I was down in Berkeley we never used wire, we weren't allowed to 'cos of the hunting, and we managed all right."

One day, when he was in the shop, he noticed my bandaged hand. On learning that I had a septic finger, he said, "When I was down in Dorset, I knew a man who had a finger go septic from a gooseberry thorn, just like your finger. He was dead in four days."

"Don't you take any notice of him," Father told me, when Cordwell had left the shop. "How do he know what your finger's like, with all that bandage on it? You don't never want to take much notice of what they cross-country chaps say."

Father hadn't much opinion of "cross-country chaps". A person who'd come from some distance, especially one who had a reputation for always moving, was a "cross-country chap". And, Father reasoned, it was because they were not much good that they had, perforce, to move. "It stands to reason," he often said, "if they were any good, they'd stand their ground, but they bain't and then when folks find them out for what they are, they've got to move on."

CHAPTER
TWO

"Alle manner of men"

WM. LANGLAND

The farmers wore breeches and leggings. Their workaday breeches were of a hardwearing twill or cord, and the leggings were black leather. Their boots were stout, nailed and black.

Some of the older farmworkers also wore breeches and leggings, but all the farmworkers wore heavy black hob-nailed boots. Few wore rubber wellington boots except on the wettest of days. Most farmworkers wore corduroys or similar tough trousers, bought from Mr Pemberthy's Emporium. For several years now Mr Pemberthy had stocked blue overalls and these had become quite popular with many of the younger farmworkers. He'd also stocked breeches and trousers made of another material which looked and felt hardwearing, but several buyers said these went into holes within a fortnight. They complained, or at least their wives did. Not many farmworkers actually went into the shops and bought their own clothes, the wives did their shopping. Mr Pemberthy tried reasoning with them, putting forward a multitude of excuses, but to no avail. The women said, "If that's your attitude, we'll get our clothes in town." Mr Pemberthy refunded most of their money and stopped stocking breeches and trousers in that material.

The Emporium sold a wide range of goods, food as well as clothes for men, women and children, and Mr Pemberthy was always on the lookout for "new lines". "Anything from a pin to an anchor, is my motto," said Mr Pemberthy. We didn't think he'd do much trade in anchors, but we knew what he meant; and from him and the other shopkeepers most of the necessities could be obtained. But Mr Pemberthy was shrewd and he'd noticed that more women were travelling by train into town, weekly, fortnightly, or monthly. So, rather than risk losing customers, he paid up when they threatened to shop in town.

Sometimes the trousers were strapped or tied with string just below the knee. Yorks, as the straps or strings were called, kept them warm above the knee, made bending or kneeling easier, and kept the trouser bottoms out of the mud. Others overcame this mud problem by tying string round the ankles or by wearing the legs of old wellingtons, or, more recently, leather anklets filched from the Home Guard stores.

Boots were the only things the men actually went into the shop and bought themselves. Everybody went to Mr Teakle's boot and shoe shop on the corner. The heavy nailed boots were called boots, the lighter boots with no nails were called shoes, and shoes were called low shoes, or more generally by farmworkers "tea-drinkers", but not many ever wore these.

Mr Teakle had pairs of boots of all shapes and sizes hanging up in his shop. The shapes varied according to how much the boots were sprung. "These," said Mr Teakle, reaching up with his stick to unhook a pair from the ceiling, "are three-quarters sprung. There," putting them on the counter. "And these," reaching up with the stick again, "are slightly sprung." The slightly sprung are placed beside the three-quarter sprung. "Over here," Mr Teakle limps over to the far corner and unhooks another pair, "are some fully sprung." Fully sprung are also placed on the counter. "Ah. Now just a minute," says Mr Teakle, "just let me get that other pair down, just to show you." The fourth pair are put beside the others. Mr Teakle wipes his hands on his apron and breathes rather heavily. He was gassed during the 1914-18 war, his own son is fighting in this one and Mr Teakle has had no news for months and months. In fact it has been so long that we no longer like to ask about him.

"I just wanted you to see these," Mr Teakle said when his breathing was more normal, "made of the finest horsehide, last for ever if they're well looked after. Everybody should have at least three pairs of boots, so that they can let them dry out and dubbin them. They should never be dried out by the fire and they must be dubbined regularly." Mr Teakle paused and sighed before saying, "More boots are ruined by neglect, than are ever worn out." He looked down at his blackened, outstretched hands and grinned ruefully. "A lot of the beggars only dubbin 'em when they bring 'em to me to repair. Now these," he said pointing to the third pair he'd placed on the counter, "are fully sprung. Notice how much more the toes are off the ground than the three-quarters sprung, and how much more again than these slightly sprung, See?" He jabbed a forefinger at the slightly sprung. "Hardly turned up at all, while the fully sprung are quite three and a half inches. Fully sprung are made for those who do a lot of hill walking. Most of those over the Forest wear but fully sprung. Shepherd's boot is another name for them."

The shop smelt of leather and wax. Leather belts with brass buckles and leather laces hung from the walls. On shelves behind the counter were leggings: black pairs and brown pairs, pairs with straps and pairs with buttons. Mr Teakle took a boot out of a cardboard box and held it lovingly by its toe and heel. "Here's a well made boot," pushing with his hands to make the boot bend slightly. "An ideal market boot, and a stout boot," letting the boot spring back, "but flexible. A good boot is the cheapest." He replaced the brown market boot in the box and started hanging up the heavy farm boots. "Of course, these farm boots need a bit of breaking in. Plenty of dubbin, that's the stuff, leather needs feeding. Farm muck is hard on them, but the biggest test of a boot is wet grass. Those rubber boots," pointing to a cluster of wellingtons suspended from a rafter, "are waterproof, but it's not wise to wear them too much. They're bad for the eyes; they prevent the electricity from the body going to earth. There's nothing like good leather for footwear. You must look after your feet; if they're uncomfortable, you'll be miserable all over. Look how sprack Dr Higgins is, always on his feet. Very funny about his shoes, I've always got to get him the good old vegetable tanned white whale. And Mr Tucker, the butcher, he always has extra soles and heels put on his new boots. 'There, Daniel,' he tells me every autumn when he buys a new pair, 'I'm set up for the winter now.'

"Years ago, when my father was alive and we made boots, the farm men would order new boots just before harvest and then, when they got their harvest money, they'd come in and get them, but today a lot of the men, especially the younger ones, go for the cheaper boot. And who can blame them, with the shockingly low wages they get, but it's false economy." Mr Teakle began to chuckle. "I remember my father making a pair of boots for your grandfather once, which I delivered. Your father and uncle were only boys then. Next day your grandfather brought the boots back into the shop and said angrily to my father, 'Look here, Daniel' — my father's name was Daniel too — 'these boots haven't got any tongues in them. Now what sort of trick do you call that?' 'They had when I made them,' said my father, inspecting the boots. 'Look here, they've been cut out!' 'Well, I'll go to see,' replied your grandfather, 'I'll make further enquiries about this.' And further enquiries revealed that your uncle had cut the tongues out to make hinges for his rabbit hutch."

Mr Teakle peered at me over the top of his pebble glasses and shook his thick mop of white hair. "How times have changed, and will. For the better in many ways. I remember the hard times and don't want to see them back. The bad old days of the workhouses and no pensions. Elderly couples lived in fear of ending their days, separated, in the grubber — as they called the workhouse. Mr Lloyd George changed all that. But when Mr Lloyd George was a rising young reformer, this village, or town as we liked to call it, was self-contained. We had a brewery, a flour mill and a rope works. Now they've all gone and so have the wheelwright and the clockmaker — that's one of his clocks." Mr Teakle pointed to the grandfather clock in the corner. "And a tailor. And my father and grandfather used to make harness, as well as boots. Gradually our village businesses are disappearing. People now look to the towns for cheap mass-produced stuff. More of us will disappear after the war, you'll see."

On market days the farmers wore breeches of a wider cut, and brown leggings. In the days of Mr Teakle's father no doubt the market breeches were made by the village tailor, but now they were made by the tailor at our market town. Mr Teakle still supplied the shining brown leather leggings.

Mr Claude Linley, as befitted the most prosperous and largest farmer, wore light-coloured breeches of the most generous cut, with buckskin strapping. His leggings were made of boxcloth and his brown boots highly polished. (Most farmers wore black boots with their brown leggings, which was, I thought, a trifle incongruous.) How grand he looked, in his brown bowler, his long dog-tooth checked jacket flowing over his breeches and his hands thrust into the cross-cut pockets of those expensive, well cut breeches. Mr Linley had a large arable acreage, and adequate implements to work it; his farm stretched into the next parish, where the ground was lighter and easier worked. He had been the only farmer to own a tractor before the war and now he had three. He also had a herd of pedigree Dairy Shorthorns, attested and milk recorded. In his large cattle yards he fattened his Shorthorn bullocks and cross-bred Herefords. And he still kept, though much reduced, a flock of Clun sheep.

"The Linleys," said other farmers, not without a trace of envy in their voices, "allus did have money, and money makes money."

He was, it must be admitted, a little out of the class of our normal working farmers. Not that he didn't work, but you never saw him covered in muck or doing any of the menial tasks. Good-natured, affable, a kindly employer, he was respected throughout the district — the countryman is always prepared to respect a gentleman who behaves like a gentleman. Mr Linley bridged the gap between farmers and that small but remote group of people known as "the gentry".

Ernest Saggamore farmed Suttridge Farm, one of the larger farms in our district. Mr Saggamore, who was a second cousin of Father's, used to farm a few miles away, just over the border in Herefordshire. He had bought Suttridge when the remains of the estate were sold a few years back. Unlike Mr Linley, Mr Saggamore hadn't been born into money, but he had the knack of making money, even when times were bad. Though he was a relative, albeit a distant one, I rarely saw him and knew little about him, except that he was reputed to be shrewd and hardworking, a man of boundless energy. He wasn't often mentioned at home. Occasionally Father would remark, "Ernest's a grafter." Or Uncle might, on his return from market, tell us, "Ernest Saggamore sent some damned good fat bullocks in today."

The Putterill sisters, Hannah and Lydia, spinsters of indeterminate age, had a smallholding adjoining Suttridge Farm on which they grew fruit and kept poultry and bees and, sometimes, a few calves. They dealt at Father's shop and every so often he received postcards from them marked URGENT in big block capitals. The messages on the cards began with, "We simply must have straight away and without delay . . ." Always written in vivid green ink, and most of the words underlined, not once, but often two or even three times, sometimes even four times. Every sentence ended with at least one exclamation mark and probably two.

"Here," Father would say to me on receipt of one of their cards, pushing the card under my nose, "you'd better jump on your bike and take this stuff over to them." The "stuff" was usually some poultry requisite, small enough for me to carry on a bicycle, or else a saw, a hammer or secateurs. The Putterill sisters were great wreckers of tools. They were also enthusiastic scytheswomen (if that is the correct term, should it perhaps be scythers, or perhaps users of a scythe?), and my trips in the summer would often be the result of an urgent call for a carborundum stone (oh, the stones those women broke, or lost), a scythe blade, a grass hook, or some wedges. In their hands, scythes and sharpening stones simply flew to pieces.

Miss Hannah, the elder one, was taller and thinner than her sister. Her hair was dark and done in a bun, and she was of rather a severe appearance until she spoke. When speaking she became animated, jabbing a stubby forefinger into the palm of the other hand to emphasise some point.

Miss Lydia had fair hair, tied back loosely with a large ribbon bow, a style far too young for her. At times she affected an arch skittishness, and giggled in a manner quite out of keeping with her years. Yet surprisingly, it was Miss Lydia who was critical of Miss Hannah's behaviour, not the other way round. Lydia never tired of saying "The trouble with my sister is that she will gossip. I say to her, "Han," I say, "I do wish you wouldn't repeat gossip." I'm always telling her, "Han, gossip will be the downfall of you one fine day, my girl. Like Humpty Dumpty, you'll fall down one fine day, Han, my girl, and all the king's horses and all the king's men, let alone little me, won't be able to help you." I tell her, but she won't harken to me, she won't be said, she's that hardened. She'll do herself a mischief one day."

"Oho," said Uncle George, when being told of this remark. "Well, I'm damned sure nobody else'll do her a mischief."

From my observations of Miss Lydia, I'd say she was every bit as much a gossip as her sister. "Have you heard the news?" Lydia would say, her hand held confidentially to the side of her mouth and her eyes all a-sparkle, "I just called in at the Post Office and overheard them talking, and accordingly . . ." Hannah would precede her gossip by, "Do you know?" in a long drawn out whisper. "Do you know? Well, seemingly . . ." As they spoke, one could mentally see certain words underlined, just like their postcards. They both had the same reaction on hearing news. A long, slow intake of breath, raised eyebrows, then, "You don't say!" And hands placed on stomachs, they'd repeat in incredulous tones, "You don't say!"

They waged an increasing war on rats, mixing red poison with lard and carefully spreading it on slices of bread, which they cut into dainty squares before distributing them to the haunts of the rats. Postcards with three URGENTS would come when they needed more rat poison: "URGENT! URGENT! URGENT! Imperative! We need more red rat poison at the very earliest!"

They wore galoshes on their smallholding, and homemade aprons, fastened at the back by large buttons. Inside their porch (choc-a-bloc with pot plants, as was their kitchen and living-room), they kept a small square mirror and comb. Even if they were only going out to their poultry, they stopped, looked in the mirror and combed wisps of hair into place, then patted their heads. In Miss Hannah's case, she adjusted her hairpins. They must, I think have had private means, as it is doubtful if their smallholding could have supported them. They seemed comfortably off, and even had a small motor car, an Austin Seven which they referred to as "Our Baby".

On my errands to the Misses Putterill, I passed Willow Farm, where Uncle George used to go and help the farmer, Mr Clutterbuck, with his haymaking, harvesting, threshing, root hoeing and hauling. Mr Clutterbuck didn't grow his mangolds "on the flat" like everyone else, but "on the ridge". Before he sowed the mangold seed the ground was set up in ridges by a bouting plough, rather in the same way that potatoes are earthed up. The seed was then sown along the top of the ridges by a drill specially made for the job.

"Bit of a caper, ain't it?" Uncle George said every year when he went to help with the singling of the mangold plants.

"The finest way to grow mangolds," was Mr Clutterbuck's annual reply.

"Helluva fiddle-faddle if you ask me," Uncle George would grunt. "If I was you, Arthur, I'd make the buggers grow on the flat like everyone else do."

But Mr Clutterbuck paid no heed to the advice. He was one of the old school of farmers. There was a right and proper way, an old, tried and proved method, and that was the only way for him. Not for him, "the newfangled nonsense preached by the professors".

"They say turnips and mangolds are nothing but water," Mr Clutterbuck said one day, removing his pipe from his mouth and spitting. "Well, I've milked cows on mangolds and fattened teas on turnips and if 'tis water — and I'm not saying 'tis," and here Mr Clutterbuck pointed the stem of his pipe at his listeners and looked gravely at them, "if 'tis only water, then 'tis damned good water." Then he put the pipe back in his mouth, and, after blowing out several huge clouds of smoke, announced, "It's my opinion them professors be in the pay of the cattle food manufacturers."

He wore breeches and leggings all the year round, and a check waistcoat from which dangled a watch chain, and over this a khaki smock. With his floppy old tweed hat and rubicund face, he couldn't possibly have been taken for anything else but a farmer. Townspeople, when feeling well disposed towards farmers, probably had somebody like Mr Clutterbuck in mind. He worked his farm with horses, and though he had enough arable to enable him to obtain a tractor, he wouldn't have one. Sometimes he was glad enough to have the War Ag with their tractors to help him to catch up on his cultivations, but he didn't really approve of them. "They churn the ground up and form a hard pan in the furrow bottom. They'll ruin the ground, you'll see."

Mr Clutterbuck had farmed his land in the old Norfolk Four Course Rotation: roots, barley, one year clover ley, wheat. The roots were sugar beet, which was sold; kale, cut and carted to the cows; and mangolds which were carted, clamped and fed to the cows and bullocks after Christmas. On the turnips and swedes the sheep were folded, their manure enriching the ground. Barley followed the roots and was undersown with ryegrass and clover seed. The following year the grass and clover were cut for hay and then ploughed in and the ground planted with wheat. When the wheat was harvested the stubble was dressed with manure from the yarded cattle. Mr Clutterbuck "farmed as though he were going to farm for a thousand years and lived as if he were going to die tomorrow", following the code of his forefathers. But despite his jovial appearance, he had the air of one who was weighted down. After the prosperous years of the last war, he moved from the farm his family had rented for generations and bought the larger Willow Farm. Farming was booming in 1919 and farms were dear. He put all the money he had into buying the farm and took up the rest from the bank. But the farming boom didn't last many years, farming profits fell and eventually disappeared altogether. The value of farmland dropped and dropped.

The banks, once so eager to lend money, began to press for earlier and larger repayments of the loans. Some farmers, by tightening their belts and adapting themselves, survived. Moneyed men like Mr Linley were able to manage; ones like Rugman became grasping. Shrewd, energetic ones like Saggamore managed, with a dash of luck, to prosper. Others were driven to despair, bankruptcy, drink, insanity, or suicide.

Mr Clutterbuck's high farming wasn't adequate for the situation, but he was stubborn, obstinate. His farming began to slip; he was forced to sell his bullocks as stores to raise a little money, instead of fattening them in his yards and making muck to dress his wheatfields. Men had to be laid off. Ditches went undug, hedges unlaid, arable fields tumbled down to grass. Brambles crept out into the fields, weeds grew in fields which had once been clean and, I suspect, they grew in Mr Clutterbuck's heart.

Only the rabbits prospered.

The bank grew more persistent and the time came when Mr Clutterbuck couldn't find any more money. All he wanted was peace of mind and to be allowed to stop at Willow Farm. So one day he put a horse in the gig and drove over to Herefordshire and asked Mr Saggamore to buy Willow Farm. Mr Saggamore bought it, but at a third of the price that Mr Clutterbuck had paid for it.

And even that price, considering the state of things, he was lucky to get. Mr Clutterbuck remained at Willow Farm, but his money was gone, times were hard and he only just managed to survive. And now, in the shadow of the U-boats, farming was prosperous again. But the prosperity came too late for Mr Clutterbuck, who was, despite the booming laugh, a broken man.

Once, after helping with some job or other, Mr Clutterbuck handed me a mug of sparkling cider. While I was drinking it, he said, "So you want to be a farmer?" I nodded my head. "Well, get all the education you can. They can't take that away from you." I finished my drink and read the inscription on the mug.

> Let The Wealthy And Great
> Roll In Splendour And State
> I Envy Them Not, I Declare It.
> I Eat My Own Lamb,
> My Own Chicken And Ham,
> I Shear My Own Fleece And I Wear It.
> I Have Lawns, I Have Bowers,
> I Have Fruit, I Have Flowers,
> The Lark Is My Morning Alarmer,
> So Jolly Boys Now
> Here's God Speed The Plough,
> Long Life And Success To The Farmer.

Soon after Mr Clutterbuck had sold his farm the estate was put up for sale. The old squire had sold off a farm or a house from time to time, but a few years after his death the whole estate was put up for sale. The farms were first offered to the tenants. A few bought them, but not so many, they hadn't the money. The estate was auctioned; some farms tenanted and some with vacant possession. Mr Saggamore bought the vacant Suttridge Farm. Some farms sold for as little as ten pounds an acre, while others were on the market for years. Hardly anybody wanted the tenanted farms at any price, though I believe Mr Saggamore bought one or two of the smaller outlying farms. Most of the others remained unsold until shortly before the beginning of the war. Even now it was doubtful if some of them had been paid for. "I know for a fact," Uncle George was wont to declare, "that Len Wilson ain't paid a penny piece for his farm until this very day."

Houses and cottages were also hard to sell. A good, solid little house could be bought for a little over a hundred pounds.

The Hall itself remained unsold and unoccupied until September 1939, when it was rapidly converted into a hostel for Land Army girls.

CHAPTER
THREE

"And to be a farmer's boy"

Farming was in the news, to judge by the spate of articles in the papers and the number of farming books being published. Most of the writers of these were observers, and some not very accurate observers either.

Journalists discovered that the straw-chewing yokels of yesteryear were sagacious, exemplary characters. Politicians called them the salt of the earth. Country broadcasters' accents became thicker. A dozen writers wrote records of "a remote year in the country". Some wrote of "the meditations in peace and strife in the fields". Businessmen, lately turned farmers, rushed into print to tell of their farming successes. One such man wrote a series of books in rapid, too rapid, succession, extolling his farming success. Anyone could farm successfully, he proclaimed, with a text book. But I suspected his business bank balance may have helped him too. I would have liked to see Mr Clutterbuck pointing his pipe at him and telling him a thing or two. It wasn't quite as these people told it. Farming was fashionable. And essential, as the Women's Land Army song explained:

"Back to the Land, with its clay and sand,
Its granite and gravel and grit,
You grow barley and wheat
And potatoes to eat
To make sure that the nation keeps fit . . ."

Farmers were told to produce more milk, potatoes, wheat, oats and barley. All our sugar was home-produced from sugar beet. The call-up of farmworkers was postponed. More and more land came under the plough: six million acres more than there was in 1939 — almost as much as in farming's heyday eighty years earlier.

The War Ag ordered every farmer to plough. Both large and small farmers were required to plough their allotted share. For the farmer who already had arable land this was not such a problem, but the all-grassland farmer had no tillage or harvesting equipment. A tractor could plough two furrows quicker than horses could plough one, but tractors, like cultivators and binders, were in short supply. A permit was necessary before a tractor could be obtained and even with a permit there was a long wait.

An advertisement in the *News Chronicle* showed the state of affairs:

Owner of tractor (on H.P.) wishes to correspond with widow who owns a modern Foster thrasher; object matrimony; send photograph of machine."

The War Ag had machinery depots and did contract work for farmers; but, of course, this meant delay, farmers had to wait their turn and favourable weather conditions were often lost. Gradually, however, the green Fordson tractors appeared on the larger farms; but the sinall farmers still had to rely on the War Ag contract service or on neighbours. Their small arable acreage did not entitle them to a permit for a tractor and, in any case, their acreage would have been too small to warrant such an outlay. The only alternative to more ploughing orders was to keep more cows and this is what some farmers did. But there was no alternative to bureaucracy, directives, regulations, and restrictions. There were farm inspections by officials, much resented and feared by some, especially when they heard at secondhand that officials had been seen walking over their land. The threshing contractors had to send a return of every sack of wheat to the War Ag, and any farmer found to have sacks of undeclared wheat was in serious trouble. And behind all this was the threat of dispossession which could follow failure to comply with directives.

A farmer had no right of appeal against the War Ag. Much of its work was done in secrecy and by April 1943 there had been 2,661 dispossessions. Most farmers were well aware of the urgent need to grow the maximum amount of food and co-operated willingly, and though on the whole the Committees acted with tact and understanding the dispossessions bred a smouldering resentment which was to last a long time.

The long neglect of agriculture had to be remedied, scrubland and ditches had to be cleared. Farmers were paid two pounds for every acre of grassland they ploughed. Government subsidies were given for this and for fertilisers. The War Ag constantly encouraged the use of fertilisers. Before the war, little fertiliser, except basic slag, salt, and lime, had been used. But now almost every farmer was using sulphate af ammonia and, when they were available, sulphate of potash and phosphates.

Yes, farming was fashionable and essential and, at last, profitable, though prices were controlled; and even privileged to a certain extent. Petrol was allowed for business — and this could be made to cover a wide field. Also farmers did not suffer so much from the exigencies of food rationing. In some quarters this did not make farmers more popular.

Mrs Hatch, the village newsagent, was the most outspoken, the most virulent. But Mrs Hatch could always be relied upon in this respect. Mind you, she was playing up in her own line of business, she'd always been autocratic, but now with the shortage of newspapers and other things, she really was very trying. She wouldn't deliver newspapers any more and if anyone upset her, quite an easy thing to do, as like as not she wouldn't let them have a newspaper again. She sold several off-ration commodities, but she was choosy, capricious even, about the people she sold them to. Everything, newspapers included, was kept under the counter. She only opened the shop now for short periods when she felt like it, and it was at different times every day, and sometimes only for an hour during the day. As everyone who wanted a newspaper had to go to the shop, this arrangement was extremely awkward for the majority of her customers. But that, I believe, was her object.

Customers had tried knocking on the door of her house when the shop was closed in order to obtain their papers. They were greeted by such a frenzy of wrath that they never did it a second time.

The Bolsheviks had been her main target of attack, but since Russia had become our ally she'd gone a bit quiet about them. Farmers and especially farmers' wives became the main recipients of her venom. She railed against them in the shop, and of course with her short opening periods she nearly always had a good audience. She fulminated in the street, on the railway station and in the train. Recently she'd taken to attending church every Sunday morning and after the service she would hold forth just outside the church porch.

"Those farmers' wives think they can come and knock me up at any hour of the day or night. Of course, they've got a bit of money now, and I always said there's them as thinks that money talks. Get anything with money, some of 'em think. They've got nearly everything as it is. The Government's chuckin' money at them. I remember when some of them, not so very far away from here neither, hadn't got a shillin'. And owed people money too — some of them's got very high and mighty ways now, and I could name a few of them too, if I'd a mind to. My Ebenezer says put a beggar on horseback, that's what Ebenezer says. They gets extra clothing coupons and petrol. Lord only knows how they get the petrol to go gallivanting all over the place. And no wonder eggs and bacon are short, they eat it all themselves. Well, it oughtn't to be allowed and I've written to my M.P. about it."

But I think she most enjoyed telling a railway carriage full of startled strangers about the iniquities of farmers and their wives. For their especial benefit she would dwell on subsidies and food. She knew for a fact, she told them, that several farmers' wives spent most of their time making butter for the black market. She could name names, she said. Then there was the farmers: "what they get up to with the landgirls won't bear repeating." As the train drew into the station, Mrs Hatch (who was bound for W. H. Smith), hurriedly told them about the farmers and the petrol.

The petrol more than anything was a source of resentment with many people besides Mrs Hatch, and I must admit that the Farmers' Union meetings at the Crown never used to have a tenth of the attendance they had now. Also, a lot of farmers seemed to be going about with a few bolters of straw in their car trailers.

People who lived a long way from the church could also obtain petrol to attend services. I wonder if the vicar ever pondered on the sudden conversions since petrol rationing?

I called to see Aunt Aggie. She was Father's older sister, she was thin and wore a doleful expression and old-fashioned black clothes. Her husband, Sam Fisher, had been a decorator before the war, but now worked in a factory. It was half-past six and she was fussing about in a pair of fluffy pink slippers.

"Just sit down there by the fire," she told me. "I'm getting your Uncle Sam's tea ready for him against the time he gets home. And putting everything nice and comfy for him." She picked up a couple of brown cushions, shook them up and replaced them on the sofa. "I was going to have a read after," said Aunt Aggie (she was one of the few who read), "but now you've come we'll be able to have a nice little chat. Excuse me a moment, I must go and have a look at the broth. I gave him some beef tea last night, he liked that."

She went into the kitchen and I looked round the room. It was small and overcrowded. A large gilt-framed mirror hung over the fireplace, and underneath on the mantelshelf stood a silver-framed photograph of her with Uncle Sam standing outside the church on their wedding day. On either side of this were china ornaments, a cat, a dog and something else, I don't know what, except that it was a souvenir from Weston-super-Mare; and a china clock. In the middle of the room was a round mahogany pedestal table, rather rickety and covered with a dark green chenille cloth, heavily tasselled round the edge. Against the wall farthest from the fireplace stood a chiffonier on which a number of photographs were displayed: Uncle Sam alone, Aunt Aggie alone, Uncle Sam and Aunt Aggie together, my grandfather and grandmother, Uncle Sam's mother and father, Uncle George and Father as boys, even one of me when I was a baby. By the doorway was a large photograph of Uncle Sam when he was a young man.

Aunt Aggie returned and saw me looking at this photograph. "Wasn't he handsome in those days? Fair turned my heart over, he did." She laid a white tablecloth on top of the other one and began laying knives and forks. "Well, isn't it nice of you to come and see your old Aunty." She sat down, facing me, and stretched her legs out towards the fire. "What do you think of my slippers? Lovely, aren't they? The old fellow gave them to me for my birthday. You'll stop and have a cup of tea with us and a bit of cake. Of course you will. Now just let me put his Andrews and his iron pills and vitamin tablets out."

Aunt Aggie went into the kitchen and came back with a jug of water and two glasses. She sat down again, her breath smelling of whisky. "George tells me you want to work on a farm. I don't expect your Mother likes that." She looked pensive for a moment and then continued, "It's hard work on a farm and you don't look very strong. Where are you going to work?"

"I'd like to go to Mr Clutterbuck's."

"George says he's very nice, but I don't know him, I don't get about very much. Your mother goes to the whist drives, doesn't she? And the Women's Institute?" She went out and came back with a pair of long woollen underpants which she draped over a high-backed chair, placing it near the fire. "I bought Sam a new shirt the other day. Very skimpy, clothes are these days. It was hardly long enough to cover his possible. He likes his shirts long so that he can tuck them between his old legs. His legs have got ever so small." Aunt Aggie put on her "end of the world" look and said, "It all worries me, your Uncle Sam's health, this terrible war. I don't think it'll ever end, we'll all get blown to smithereens, I think. And poor Mr Teakle, I don't think he'll ever see his son again. And Mr Jones' son, those terrible Germans have got him. And the vicar, he's failing fast, and I should think those Adney children have got consumption. Then there's the rationing, it's a job to keep body and soul together. And all the terrible things you read about in the paper. And all these girls going about with Yanks — I think I can smell Sam's dinner burning!" She scuttled off into the kitchen, returning a few moments later.

The china clock on the mantelpiece chimed seven. "Your Uncle Sam'll be home." Aunt Aggie poked the fire and shovelled on some more coal, which she got out of a large brass coal box with a hinged lid. Then she began to rearrange the antimacassars on the easy chairs and pummelled and banged the cushions on the sofa. "His slippers! His slippers! I quite forgot his slippers." She rushed out of the room and returned in a few minutes, looking slightly flustered and carrying a pair of very worn leather slippers in her left hand. In her right hand she carried an earthenware bed warmer. "That's talking for you," she said, as she put the slippers and the bed warmer in the hearth. "Now the kettle." She brought the kettle from the kitchen and placed it on the hob.

"That's his chair you're sitting in, you'd better move into that other one." She gave the cushions in his chair a thorough flouncing and rearranged the arm covers. A newspaper was placed on the one arm and a padded foot stool put in front of the chair.

"There, that's all ready for him, though sometimes he likes to flop on the sofa. Dreadful job about the newspapers, isn't it? Mrs Hatch is very difficult. I don't like going there, she's that impudent. I wouldn't go there, but Sam likes his paper and the old fellow don't have much."

The kettle began to boil and Aunt Aggie filled the bedwarmer with water. "I'll just take this up and pop it into the bed. I wrap his nightshirt round it and put his nightcap and bedsocks under it. His poor old head and feet feel the cold you know, something terrible." The bedwarmer was taken upstairs and the kettle refilled and placed on the hob. "He'll be here any minute now. I'll turn the lamp down, he doesn't like too much light, it hurts his poor old eyes." We heard a knocking on the front door and Aunt Aggie said excitedly, "There he is. Go and let him in while I warm the pot and make the tea. I always bolt the door, because you never know."

I unbolted the door — actually there were four bolts and a chain to undo — and let Uncle Sam in. I followed him into the living-room. Aunt Aggie hastily put the tea-pot on the table and covered it with a tea-cosy, then she bounded up to Uncle Sam, flung her arms round his neck and kissed him loudly and heartily. When she'd finished, Uncle Sam staggered back a pace and waggled his head. Aunt Aggie removed his bowler hat, took his gas mask, which had been hanging from a long strap on his shoulder, and placed these carefully on an upright chair. She then began to help him remove his raincoat, while he managed to remove his woollen gloves and scarf unaided. Thus divested, Uncle Sam bent over the fire and began rubbing his hands.

Aunt Aggie went into the kitchen and returned with two bowls of steaming broth. She mixed a glass of

Andrews Liver Salts. "Here you are, Sam, drink this down while it's still fizzy."

"All right, Aggie, but I'll let it quieten down a bit. You know I don't like it too fierce."

"It won't do you any good if you don't drink it while it's fizzy, Sam," she said, and turning to me, "it gets up his nose and he don't like that." Uncle Sam screwed up his face and swallowed the salts.

"There's a good boy," said Aunt Aggie, handing him a glass of water and some pills. "Here, swallow your iron pills, put some iron into your system. Hurry up, your broth is getting cold, it won't do you much good if it's only lukewarm." Aunt Aggie handed me a cup of tea and a slice of cake on a plate and then she and Uncle Sam sat down at the table.

"Got any appetite tonight, Sam?"

"Mm, mm, mm," mumbled Uncle Sam, between mouthfuls of broth.

"Coax yourself a bit, Sam, my dear."

"Mm, mm, mm."

"Did you manage to go at work?" asked Aunt Aggie, and in a confidential whisper to me, "He couldn't open his bowels before he went to work this morning, so I told him to have a good try later on."

Aunt Aggie looked at him anxiously and asked, "You were careful, weren't you, Sam?"

She looked at me and said, "It's this V.D. they keep warning us about in the papers. I don't rightly know what it is, but I think it's one of those things you don't talk about, but they say in the papers you catch it off lavatory seats. Dreadful, isn't it? This war has brought some terrible things going about, hasn't it? Those nasty squander bugs and suchlike."

Uncle Sam was tucking into his big bowl of broth, three times the size of Aunt Aggie's. There didn't seem to be much the matter with his appetite.

"Don't chom, Sam. Whatever will our visitor think? Besides, it's ever so bad for your digestion. Look how you had the colly-wobbleys the night before last." Uncle Sam belched and Aunt Aggie said, "That's right, Sam, get rid of that nasty old wind." Uncle Sam's moustache was dripping with broth. Aunt Aggie started to titter. "Look at his old moustache. He, he, he, isn't it comical? Oh, I know I shouldn't laugh. Now, now, Sam, try not to sneeze, you'd make such a mess."

Aunt Aggie picked up the empty dishes. Uncle Sam had made a good tidy job of his by rubbing bread round and round it. "There, you've made a good job of that, Sam." Uncle Sam was still pulling and chewing at the bread. She showed me the empty bowl. "There, look, he's eaten every morsel. Broth is so nourishing. You want to get your Mother to make some for you, you look as if you could do with it."

A fried egg and two black-looking sausages were placed in front of Uncle Sam. "That's the best I could do, Sam. Now, don't gollop it, you know what it does to your poor old tummy." Aunt Aggie insisted on giving me another cup of tea. "You have another cup. I've got plenty of tea, your Uncle George brought it. He gets it from that black market place people talk so much about. I wish he could get me some proper sausages, there's only bread in the ones you get now, and a bit of gristle to give it some reality. It's my belief they put sawdust in them."

Uncle Sam had finished his sausages and egg and was busy rubbing bread round his plate.

"Sam, you never put your slippers on."

"I'll put them on in a mo, Aggie."

"Here, have a bit of cake for afters."

Uncle Sam munched away at his cake while Aunt Aggie knelt down by the table and untied his bootlaces. She eased his boots off and put his slippers on his feet. He grunted a "thank-you" and started to pour tea from his cup into his saucer.

"What sort of a day did you have at the factory, Sam?"

"So-so — splurp — very so-so — splurp," he replied, sucking tea out of his saucer.

"He don't say much about his work at the factory, it's hush-hush." Aunt Aggie began clearing the table and I began thinking of an excuse to leave. Uncle Sam blew his nose long and hard, and carefully inspected his handkerchief before putting it back in his pocket. He got up from the table and stretched himself out on the sofa. Soon he was snoring loudly. Aunt Aggie put a finger to her lips and whispered, "I think you'd better go now, your Uncle's tired. Come another day and perhaps he'll sing you one of his comic songs." On tip-toe she led me along the passage. Uncle Sam's coat, gas mask and bowler hat were hanging up in the passage with his Air Raid Warden's helmet and whistle. Uncle Sam was an Air Raid Warden, but he didn't do much in that line now, though at the beginning of the war he'd been very keen.

"Goodbye, and thank you for coming," Aunt Aggie whispered in the doorway. "Remember me to your mother." She closed the door behind me and I heard the four bolts slide home.

Walking home I met Reuben Kimmins and Colonel Biggs, two of Uncle George's boon companions, just about to enter the White Lion. Both were slightly disreputable and rather unreliable. Before the war, Reuben had combined jobbing building with poaching; Colonel — a nickname only — had kept a few pigs and done odd jobs. Since the war they'd had regular employment with the War Ag, Reuben as a rat catcher, and Colonel as a tractor driver. Their regular employment was a source of surprise and amusement to them. "They've got all us old odd-jobbers workin' reg'lar, bloody marvellous ain't it," they often remarked.

"You ought to stop at school and take more interest in your studies, and pass your exams. And try to get a job in a bank and then one day you might become a bank manager like your Aunt Dorothea's husband. Just think how proud I should be," said my mother, a few days later.

"I don't want to be a bank manager, Mother," I replied.

"It's a respectable occupation, and clean. And you get a pension when you retire," said Mother.

"Another cup of tea please, Ethel," said Father.

"And why don't you say something to him, Father? Tell him he must stop at school and persevere with his lessons and try to get on in the world."

"It's no good, Ethel. The boy's made up his mind."

"Huh!" snorted Mother. "He doesn't know his own mind, how can he at his age? He should do as he's told and stop at school."

"All this book learning's no good to them. I've seen them at his school, great lumps of boy chaps. They ought to be out earning their own living. Makes them as soft as pap, keeping them at school so long." Father, in common with most country people, had no great opinion of books.

"I had hoped he would grow up respectable and be a credit to me," sniffed Mother.

"He don't seem to have his mind on his lessons, Ethel."

"No, he doesn't. More's the pity. I've told him times out of number, but he won't listen to me, he won't be said. He's that hardened. You should have been firmer with him."

"Oh, Mother —" I said.

"Now, just you be quiet for once. You've vexed me enough as it is. You won't persevere with your schoolwork. You'll stick your nose in some trashy book, but you won't learn anything useful."

"There you are then, Ethel," said Father. "He's wasting his time at school. You've said yourself he's not interested in his lessons."

"And whose fault is that, may I ask? It's that George's fault."

"That's right. Blame our George. Nothing can ever go wrong here, but what you blame that poor old bagger."

"Well, it's right isn't it? The misery that cratur's brought me. I knew it, I knew no good would come of letting him be forever in that George's company. Now come on, haven't I said it, over and over again?"

But Father had taken refuge behind the *Daily Mail* and did not answer.

"Haven't I said it? Haven't I warned you?" persisted Mother. "Oh, why don't you get your head out of that newspaper and answer me?"

No reply came from Father.

"Answer me!" demanded Mother.

"Answer your mother, there's a good boy," said Father, his head still behind the newspaper.

"It's you I'm speaking to, Father," shouted Mother.

"Eh? What's that, Ethel?" asked Father, peering from behind the newspaper. "What's that you say?"

"I'm talking about that George."

"Oh ah," said Father, putting his paper aside and glancing up at the clock on the mantelpiece. "I'm glad you reminded me, our George'll be here directly. Put the kettle on."

"What?" screeched Mother. "He's coming here again tonight? I thought I'd be free of him tonight. He's here every whipstitch. When he comes through that door I shall put my hat and coat on and be off."

"Don't be like that, Ethel. George won't like it."

"I don't care if he likes it or not, he can lump it for all I care."

"He might be offended."

"Offended? Him?" Mother couldn't keep the amazement out of her voice, perhaps she didn't even try. "You have the gall to sit there and tell me that he may be offended. Don't you realise I've been trying to offend that cratur for the last seventeen years? But he's that hardened, he must have a skin like a rhinoceros."

Father returned to his newspaper and Mother just sat there with her knees very close together and glowered.

"You shan't come and play in our yard,
You won't swing on our apple tree,
If you're not good to me —"

Mother sat bolt upright, her body stiffened and her eyes widened like saucers. "Hark!" she said. "It's that George and he's drunk. I'm off!"

"I shouldn't do that, Ethel."

"Oh. And why not?"

"We were going to discuss the boy's future."

"In that case, I'm stopping," snapped Mother. "But why should he have any say in it?"

"He is the boy's uncle."

"He's his ruination, I'm afraid."

"Wherever in the world is he?" asked Father, turning round and looking puzzled. "He should be here by now."

"How do you expect me to know where he is? I hope he's gone to Jericho, but he's more likely to have fallen down where he's so drunk."

"Why do you suppose he's drunk?"

"Because he's singing. That's why."

"You don't have to be drunk to sing. That's your trouble, Ethel, you don't ever sing, nor you don't laugh enough. You go about looking that miserable."

"And you'd look evil if you had put up with what I've got to put up with. I sometimes think I shall go clean out of my mind, I can't put up with much more of it."

42

"We were always singing and laughing in our fambly."

"Oh. And what about that sister of yours? I can't believe that miserable object ever did much singing or laughing."

"Our Aggie could sing like a bird when she was younger."

"And she drinks like a fish now she's older."

"That she never does! Not a drop have ever passed her lips!"

"Well, all I can say is her nose and her complexion tell lies."

"You've never forgiven our Aggie, have you?"

"Not after the things she said about me. No, I have not."

"I'm damned if I can fathom wherever our George have got to."

"He'll turn up. Bad pennies always do."

"It's a damned queer thing. I'll just step outside and see if I can see if he's all right." Father suddenly looked worried and frightened and muttered, "Heart attack. Fatal, fatal."

After Father had gone outside, Mother said, "The times I've prayed the ground would open up and swallow him. I ought to go to church more often."

Father returned after a few minutes looking puzzled. "I can't see hide nor hair of him. I hope nothing's happened to him, there's some bad baggers got about these days. I was only reading in the *News of the World* about some of them the other day."

"Pah!" Mother snorted. "You and that George, filling your heads with scandals and murders. I've no patience with you."

But just then Uncle George arrived.

"Wherever have you been, George? We heard you some time ago," asked Father.

"I suddenly remembered I had a letter in me pocket so I went back to the Post Office to post it."

"Took you long enough," snapped Mother.

"And then I saw Reuben and Colonel, and so I popped into the Lion to have a drink with them," explained Uncle.

"Oh, those two good for nothings," said Mother.

"And I saw Mrs Peabody on her way to the spinney to meet her fancy chap," rumbled Uncle George mischievously.

"Never! never! I'll never believe it," said Mother, stamping her foot.

"Go and see for yourself, Ethel," advised Uncle George.

Father scraped his chair nearer to the fire and remarked, "Bit parky tonight, George."

"Ah," said Uncle. "That don't make no difference to 'em."

"Don't make no difference to who, George?" asked Father.

"Why, them up in the spinney," answered Uncle. "Quite a few on 'em do get up there. Reuben calls it the night shift."

"There's some bad baggers about," observed Father gloomily.

"I won't stop in here to listen to it," exclaimed Mother.

"Let's talk about the boy here, now we're all together," suggested Father.

"I think he ought to stop at school," said Mother.

"Aye, Ethel, we know what you think," replied Father.

"Let'n be a farmer, it's a man's life," said Uncle.

"It's his future I'm thinking about," said Mother.

"Damn it, Ethel, that's what we be talking about," retorted Father.

"There's no pension on the end of it," said Mother.

"He ain't started work yet. He'd be a funny boy if he chose his job on what he might or might not get in fifty years' time," replied Father.

"It is a consideration," said Mother.

"Let'n be a farmer," grunted Uncle George. "He's a good boy with stock and with growing things."

"We've had enough of this haggling these past few weeks. Now I'm going to give my opinion," said Father firmly. "I had once hoped as he'd come in with me in the shop. But that don't signify. George's and my father were a baker, but I didn't follow him. George did, and he didn't care all that much for the job. Let the boy please hisself, it's his life and if he wants to learn to be a farmer, well, I bain't gwain to stop him."

"Hear, hear," said Uncle George. "Let'n be a farmer."

"It's hard work," sighed Mother.

"He've done enough work on a farm to know that," replied Father.

"A farm labourer. What will Mrs Peabody say?" asked Mother.

"Pop up the spinney and ask her, Ethel," suggested Uncle George.

"Now, our George," said Father. "But after what we've heard about her tonight, I don't know as her's the sort of person whose opinion I should value."

"It's not right. It's just one of George's cock and bull stories," protested Mother.

"Let's leave Mrs Peabody out of it for once," said Father. I'd never seen Father quite so firm as this before.

"I don't know whatever Dorothea will have to say," said Mother.

"No more do I," said Father. "And I ain't ever said this afore. You be always on a carping about George here and our Aggie, but I hold my tongue. But, I'm telling you now, I don't care what the devil your Dorothea do think."

"Oh, oh," sniffed Mother, near to tears.

Uncle George refilled his pipe. Father brought Mother a glass of sherry and told her to cheer up. Uncle pushed his tobacco pouch in his pocket and withdrew it again together with an envelope, which he shyly gave to Mother. "Here you are, Ethel, I almost forgot. A few clothing dockets for you."

She mumbled thanks to Uncle George, who said, "Well, that's all settled," and leant back and lit his pipe.

"It's not much of a future," said Mother. "We'll never have enough to set him up as a farmer."

"Don't you worry about that, Ethel," mumbled Uncle George. "You won't ever need to worry about him. I got no chick nor child of me own. Well, I don't know, I always thinks of him as me own. Him and me bin butties since he were knee high to a grasshopper. Don't you worry about him, Ethel. I'll see he's all right when the time do come."

"Well, well, that's good on you, George. Ain't that good on our George, Ethel? Our George have turned up trumps," cried Father. "Thank your uncle, m'boy."

Before I could speak, Uncle George waved his hand. "There's no need for you to say anything. We're butties, you an' me, allus have bin and allus will be."

"Thank you, George," said Mother quietly. There were tears in her eyes. "I'll go and put the kettle on."

Mother went into the kitchen and Uncle George puffed at his pipe. Father kept muttering, "Good on you, George."

"Well, that's all settled," said Uncle George, a little later. "Good old stick, Clutterbuck, he'll be happy working there."

"Eh? What's that?" asked Father.

"I said, he'll be happy working at Clutterbuck's," said Uncle George.

"Who said he was going to work for Clutterbuck?" asked Father.

"Well I thought —" "That's where —" Uncle George and I spoke together.

"No, no, no. That won't do," said Father.

"Why not? Clutterbuck's all right," said Uncle George.

"Oh ah," said Father. "Clutterbuck's all right, one of the best. A good-living man too."

"Well then, what's the matter with Clutterbuck's?" asked Uncle George. "Arthur Clutterbuck have bin a furst class farmer in his time."

"That's right, George. You got it right there," replied Father.

"Soak me bob, if I have," said a puzzled Uncle George.

"You said, Arthur Clutterbuck's been a good farmer in his time," said Father patiently.

Uncle George took the pipe out of his mouth and rubbed his chin. As usual, he needed a shave, and as he rubbed he made a rasping sound. "That's right," he said, more puzzled than ever; and so was I for that matter. "There's none that can deny that Arthur Clutterbuck has bin a furst class farmer in his time."

"That's just it," explained Father. "In his time, but this ain't his time, he's behind the time. The boy's got to go somewhere to learn to farm in the modern way, in the way to make money."

"Claude Linley's up with the times, he've got all the new-fangled stuff," said Uncle George.

Mother had returned and was pouring out tea. "Well, at least Mr Linley's a gentleman," she said.

"Ah, that's just his trouble," said Father. "The man's all right, but he's never really had to make money, he's always had it. He runs his farm absolutely top-hole, but he's what I call a gentleman farmer. But the boy'll have to be a working farmer. I heard that fellow with the squeaky voice talking on the wireless the other day about dirty-boot farmers. He said it as though it were something to be ashamed of. I should have thought it were something to be proud of."

"Well, that narrows the field a bit," said Uncle George. "Some on 'em ain't much bottle. Arch Rugman f'rinstance. Cordwell's like a fly in a jam jar and old Burridge is all cackle and shit. But there's some good 'uns about. I shall have to give it some thought."

"I've given it some thought," Father said quietly "Ernest Saggamore's the man."

"You might have summat there," said Uncle George, after a moment's thought.

"But he's so uncouth," said Mother.

"He do know how to make a go on't," said Father.

"You're right there," agreed Uncle George.

"Well, Father, you know best I suppose," said Mother. Mother, despite her tantrums, always obeyed Father in the end.

"I've spoken to Saggamore and he's agreed to have you," Father told me and added, "And if you ain't willing to go to Saggamore's farm, you don't go to any farm."

CHAPTER
FOUR

"The Hoeing and the hay"

"For some delights in haymaking, and some they fancies mowin', But of all the trades as I likes best, give I the turmut-hoein'."

Traditional.

We were hand hoeing the roots. I had been at Suttridge Farm for almost six months. Some days I thought I knew Mr Saggamore and other days I did not. "This is a good king and that is a bad king," I had been told at school. That simple summing up may have been all very well for kings, but it was far from adequate with a lot of the people I knew, and especially so in the case of Mr Saggamore. One day he would be jovial, another gloomy; placid, gentle sometimes, and at other times, a veritable, raging demon. Particularly disconcerting were the times when he calmly announced, in a reasonable, almost friendly fashion, that he intended to quarrel and then proceeded to do so in a most virulent manner.

He was not unlike Father in stature, in fact I could trace several faint similarities, although they were only distant cousins. Like Father, he was slim and wiry, though a shade taller. His breeches and leggings revealed the bandiness of his short little legs.

Quite uncharacteristic of Father was his bustling energy. This was the most constant energy; never had I met anyone with such terrific and untiring enthusiasm for work. He never seemed to tire. At the end of the day he would be working as quickly and darting about as fast as he was at the beginning of the day. And after everyone else had finished, I knew that he would still be busy until dark.

Though he had a small herd of milking cows, he really despised dairy farmers. The pre-war years had driven him, like many other farmers, into milk. But his heart was in arable, beef and sheep farming. "I never did have much opinion of a man who always had a bucket in his hand," he told me on numerous occasions. He was referring to dairy, pig and poultry farmers, whose work, of course, entailed the almost continuous carrying of buckets. He reserved his special contempt for the poultry farmers. It was all right for Martha his wife, and other farmers' wives and daughters, and women such as the Putterill sisters to keep poultry. Poultry keeping was a woman's job, but for a man to do it, well, I think he thought it was almost indecent.

"To see a grown man going about with a little bucket on his arm, feeding a few fowls and going 'Coop, coop, coop', well it gives me the creeps."

He was a great reader of the *Daily Mail*, and sometimes in the afternoons he expounded on the leading article which he had assiduously studied at dinner time. Every bit of it was gospel to him and we would get quite a sermon. He read with some difficulty, moving his lips and whispering each word to himself.

Caleb Pocock was the titular cowman, though in practice Mr Saggamore, Jack Musgrove and Bill Lugg did almost as much milking as Caleb did. All the milking was done by hand. Caleb was scornful of my tyro efforts: "Thee'll never learn to milk with thee hands dry. Squirt some milk on 'em first and then squeeze and let yer finger and thumb slip down the cows' tits."

All of them milked "wet-handed". The milk would form round their fingers and thumbs into a chocolatey mess and drip from the palms of their hands. Thick crusts of it grew on the legs of their stools.

Caleb was an oldish man, near to retirement; he spent most of his time messing round the cowshed and other buildings. Another of his jobs was looking after the pigs. He wore breeches and leggings and his legs were bowed like hoops. Jack Musgrove never tired of telling us, in Caleb's absence, that "a damned great sow had once run between Caleb's legs". His greasy, cunning old face dripped with falseness, you could almost see it physically dripping like sweat. The old chap could be very plausible, with his smile and wheedling voice, and if that didn't serve his purpose, he would begin to cry and hold his hands together in a gesture of prayer.

"He's an old rascal," Mr Saggamore told me. "When I bought this place he came to see me to ask me to keep him on. I hesitated for a moment and old Caleb dropped to his knees, held his hands up praying and with tears streaming down his face, begged me to give him a job.

Then the first morning he started work, he was so anxious to please he got over-excited, hopping and jumping about, and he fell in the gubben hole, bucket and all. There was a good stack of firewood near the pigsties and I happened to see him chucking pig muck all over it, but I didn't let on, I bided my time and wondered what his game was. About a week later he said to me, 'I see that firewood's all covered in pig muck, Mr Saggamore. A gentleman like you wouldn't have any use for wood that's all covered in pig muck, now would you, Sir? Mrs Saggamore, bless 'er 'eart, wouldn't like that, would she? I'll tell you what, Sir, I'll take it off yer 'ands, Sir. A poor man like me can't afford to be too proud about a bit of pig muck. But it's different with you, Sir, and there's dear Mrs Saggamore to consider.'"

I asked Mr Saggamore what he'd done about Caleb and the firewood.

"I gave it to him, I've got a soft spot for the old rascal."

I've seen Caleb wringing his hands and muttering about how poor he was, but I've also heard him saying of anyone who'd recently upset him, "I've got more money than that bugger'll ever 'ave."

His two grown-up sons, married with families of their own, were terrified of upsetting him. "I darsen't do that," they'd say, "our old man 'ave told us, that if we don't do as 'e do soy, 'im'll cut us out of 'is will."

Caleb Pocock was tightfisted. He'd chase Bill Lugg all round the farmyard for a match to light his pipe, thereby saving one of his own. Twice I saw him bring a great wad of notes on a Friday morning and ask Bill to count them for him.

Poor Bill Lugg wouldn't have a penny by Thursday morning. Bill was unmarried, he lived over at Twistleton. Jack Musgrove said some old women at Twistleton had all his money off him in the Bull over at Twistleton on Saturday nights. "They make a bit of a fuss of him and he gets buying them port. They might let him have a little go now and then, but who'd want old Bill? He's as hairy as an ape and when he gets warm he stinks like a fitcher."

Bill Lugg was short and as strong as an ox, and Jack Musgrove was quite right, Bill was hairy. I've never seen anyone with so much hair: his hands, arms, and his chest and back were covered with thick black hair. It curled up from his chest and back right over the top of his shirt. I don't know how his barber knew where to begin or finish.

Bill was the carter, but he much preferred driving the tractor. Mr Saggamore played up to this, he would give Bill a list of jobs and then say, "— and when you've done that, Bill, I want you to do a bit of tractor driving." Bill would work like billy-o and do the jobs in double quick time so that he could do that tractor driving before Mr Saggamore changed his mind. Mr Saggamore did change his mind sometimes and poor Bill was crestfallen and would keep muttering, "'im told I, I could do some tractor work, ay 'im did. An' now 'im wunt let I drive the bugger, no 'im wunt."

"Old Bill always falls for that wet talk," Jack Musgrove would remark.

Jack Musgrove was short and stocky; his special skills were hedge laying and thatching. He also did most of the tractor ploughing. Mr Saggamore did some, but, I suspected, sitting on a tractor was not active enough for him. Bill, though he longed to do the tractor ploughing, was rarely allowed to do so, "It's no good to let Bill do it, he won't go in or out straight at the end of the furrows. And I certainly ain't going to let him do any by the road, he gets on that tractor with a fag on the go and his one arm on the mudguard, and I don't know if he goes to sleep or if it's the bacca smoke what gets in his eyes, but he gets the furrows like a dog's hind leg. I ain't having that alongside the road, with everybody looking over the hedge, I should be the laughing stock of the district. And look at that time he drove into the ditch. Took three horses and all of us half a day to get the tractor out. What made him do a thing like that, I should like to know, Jack?"

"That's where he gets so full of himself because he's driving the tractor. He starts showing off by the roadside and starts doing didows and he don't look where he's going," answered Jack.

"He's a wonderful chap for some hard slogging," said Mr Saggamore.

"Ah, but he ain't got much up in Lizzie's room. Strong in the arm, but soft in the head, that's old Bill."

We were working by the roadside now, hoeing the roots. We'd been out in the root field for weeks. As soon as the seedlings could be seen in the drills we'd horse-hoe them between the rows. I led the horse and Mr Saggamore steered the hoe. Occasionally he would bellow, "Look what you're doing, you're letting the horse step on the plants." We would hardly reach the end of the rows before Mr Saggamore started to shout, "C'mon, c'mon, turn the hoss round, don't stop there dawdling, we ought to be halfway back up the row by now. Look out! Look out! You're letting the hoss step over the chain."

Next we singled the sugar beet and then the mangolds. The plants grew in a thick and continuous line and we had to chop out the unwanted plants to leave a distance of ten inches between the beet and about twelve inches for the mangolds. The roots grew in groups, because the "seeds" were really clusters of seed. The mangolds were not so bad, but the beet was the very devil, the tiny plants twisted round each other. Every so often I would bend down and pull the plants out because they were so intertwined. Mr Saggamore maintained that a good hoer should not have to do this, every unwanted plant should be knocked out by the hoe. The sight of the drooping plants we left and the wilting plants and weeds lying in between the rows looked distressing, but the singled plants perked up in a day or two.

I learnt an important lesson while hoeing. Those who finished their rows first did not rush off and start a fresh one, but turned round and helped the others to finish their rows.

A file was kept at the end of the rows and whilst Mr Saggamore was waiting for the others to sharpen their hoes he would go to the hedge and urinate.

"Hah," said Bill Lugg on one occasion, "he've made a proper 'abit o' that. I knowed 'im go dree times in ten minutes."

"Do you remember last year when we had a landgirl helping us and we hadn't got a wood handy like we have in this field and he wet his breeches?" asked Jack Musgrove.

Mr Saggamore must have suspected by our muted voices that we were talking about him because he turned his head. "Dr Higgins once told me," wagging his bottom about, "to have a run out as often as possible, it prevents your waterworks seizing up."

I suspected the real reason was because he couldn't bear to be inactive for a moment. Had he started a row without us it would have been a breach of hoeing etiquette.

When the beet, mangolds and kale had been singled, Bill earthed up the potatoes with the bouting plough. This implement rather resembled the ordinary plough, but with a mould board each side. Nobody loved the potatoes, not even Mr Saggamore. Partly, I think, because they entailed the use of buckets; buckets to plant them and buckets to harvest them.

Again and again we horse-hoed between the rows of plants. The weather was very hot, and after a few hours of leading the horse up and down the rows my feet ached and I longed to sit down and rest under the hedge. But Mr Saggamore was remorseless, more keen than ever to be halfway back up the next row. Fiercer when I allowed the horse to step on a plant because now it was the singled plant, and if that were destroyed it would mean a gap in the row.

"C'mon, c'mon," he shouted as I neared the end of a row, "get ready to turn the hoss round. This is toppin' weather for hoss-hoeing. I love hoss-hoeing when I can see the weeds we've hoed a-sizzling in the hot sun."

Afterwards we hand-hoed between the plants in the row; this hoeing was called seconding.

"Bend your back, you can't hoe with a straight back," Mr Saggamore admonished me. My back ached as if it would split in two. It had been very different hoeing a few short rows of beetroot in Uncle George's garden from hoeing out here in this large field; hour after hour, day after day, week after week.

Tom Prewett, who had a small farm just down the road, came by, stopped and poked his blubby face over the hedge.

"Will it ever pay?" he asked Mr Saggamore.

"It's gotta bloody pay," answered Mr Saggamore, continuing the hoeing.

"It 'ouldn't do for me," said Mr Prewett.

"I like it, always been used to it," replied Mr Saggamore, still hoeing.

"It's 'ard on a poor old man," sighed Caleb.

"Too much like work for me. It's a wonder you get your chaps to stick it," said Mr Prewett.

"They don't mind it, and I'd love it," said Mr Saggamore, "and Bill do, he was brought up to it like me. Wasn't you, Bill?"

"Aye I was, Boss, that I was. I loves it, it's a good steady job," said Bill, grinning all over his face.

"Bill's a toppin' hoer, he's the only one as can keep up with me," said Mr Saggamore, pausing in his work for a moment.

Bill was highly delighted with this praise, and, after he'd lit another cigarette off the stub of the old one he'd been smoking, said, "Aye, I be."

"Well, there's no haccountin' for tastes I suppose. They made me plough up a bit of ground and grow a bit of corn an' a few taters, but I'll be glad when the war's over and I con turn it all back to grass," said Mr Prewett.

"Some on you chaps round here bent farmers at all, you be just bucket men," said Mr Saggamore.

"Thank you very much," said Mr Prewett, and went on his way.

"Chaps like that be just hindrances," said Mr Saggamore. "He don't do much work or he wouldn't be so fat. Spends most of his time going round the pubs drinking the beer up. It's because of gutsy chaps like him there ain't any beer about for the likes of us who've earned a drop."

Mr Saggamore was a complex person. One minute he'd be the hardworking, hardheaded, bustling business man, scorning anything that "didn't pay" or wasted time. Next, he'd be stopping to listen to a skylark, or rhapsodising over a thrush's song. Or parting the grass in the hedgerow bottom to enthuse over an early violet. He was passionately fond of wild flowers, often he had a primrose, bluebell, or whatever flower might be in season, dangling in the buttonhole of his jacket.

Two brothers from Twistleton came and sheared the ewes. The one, Stan, sheared the sheep and Alfie, the other, turned the handle which motivated the clippers. When Alfie slackened his speed a little, Stan shouted,

"Kip turning, Alfie. Kip turning, Alfie." Bill caught the ewes and handed them over to Stan, who held them and turned them over on to the large sheet on which he sheared them. The fleeces rolled off the sheep under Stan's expert hands. It was hard and hot work for him. He worked in a vest and the sweat rolled from his face as fast as the fleeces from the sheep.

Once they were shorn, Stan released the ewes and off they rushed, skittish without the weight of their wool. I grabbed the fleeces and rolled them up.

Mr Saggamore came and watched for a few minutes and said, "By God, Stan, you can loose 'em. I'm glad to see that wool off their backs, the fly was beginning to get on 'em."

We finished the hoeing; the leaves of the roots had grown big. "I'm glad," said Mr Saggamore, "to see the leaves cover the rows, they do quomp they old weeds."

Mr Saggamore began to get the machinery ready for haymaking. "It don't do to get the tack out at the last minute and trust to luck."

While we were oiling and checking over the machinery, he told me that before the war he had always visited the County Agricultural Show. "We used to get plenty of drink and grub given us by the merchants who exhibited there. Of course, it weren't really free, we paid for it in the long run. But I used to get as much out of them as I could, they were havin' it out o' us all the rest of the year — I'm damned if I know why these implement makers put the oil caps and adjustments in such ockerd places. It's my belief they do it on purpose — have anybody got a halfpenny?"

Jack produced a halfpenny and Mr Saggamore used it to make a larger spanner fit a smaller nut.

"Have yer father got any shiftin' spanners? If he has bring me one along tomorrow," said Mr Saggamore. "I was telling you about the show. Of course the war have put the kybosh on that job. Linley used to show some of his pedigree Shorthorns, I ain't got much time for some of these show cows, useless they be, they put it on their backs instead of in the buckets. It's a toff's job, feed 'em up to the nines. It might be different with beef animals, like Herefords, but again, I don't know. Fussed and cosseted, fed on the most expensive food. They do look very nice, but there ain't any pay in it. It'd bust an ordinary man, that caper. Here, Jack, put the jack under that wagon and get the wheels off, gawm the axles up with grease. Hey, boy, get a bent nail and get that muck out o' that oil cap afore you try to put oil in there. Look at that muntle head —"

Mr Saggamore rose to his feet and rushed across the barn towards Bill Lugg. When he came back he muttered, "The times I've told him never to smoke near the barn. Allus got a damned fag in his mouth, coughing and spluttering. I'll kill him. I believe he don't know half the time when he is smoking. Keep on dragging on them damned things all the time."

"Who's got the Brummagem screwdriver?" asked Jack. After a search the hammer was found on the floor among some loose straw.

"It's no good," said Mr Saggamore.

"He's a good 'un," said Jack.

"Who's a good 'un?" asked Mr Saggamore.

"The hammer," replied Jack. "He's a good 'un."

"I know the hammer's a good 'un," said Mr Saggamore, a little sharply.

"But you said he wasn't a good 'un," said Jack.

"Oh, that, you wasn't listening proper," said Mr Saggamore, "I said, 'It's no good,' and I meant the pedigree job ain't no good. Lose money at that caper. Sound commercial animals are the ones for vigour. Them pedigree things be too highly bred. All right for toffs to have in their parks."

"I be a crossbred. Aye, I be," said Bill, who'd come over to get a spanner. "I be 'alf Irish, I be. Some nogman in the pub called I a mongrel an' I 'it the bugger in the fizzog, aye, I did."

"I 'eard as you'd bin fightin' and quarmin' in the pub," said Jack.

"Oh, I told'n, if ever 'e called I a mongrel agen, I'd giv'n a thick ear an' all. Aye, I did," said Bill.

"You'd be surprised how ignorant some people are," said Mr Saggamore. "I met Gosworth the grocer in the Crown a while back, an' some on us was talkin' about shows. An' Gosworth said he thought the bull with the longest pissell was the champion. You'd hardly credit it would you? And Gosworth's lived in the country all his life."

"Part of the chain on the elevator's buckled," said Jack. "It wants a new piece about as long as my thing."

"Be you a champion, or just a 'ighly commended, Jack?"

"This ain't getting the work done, m'boy's, all this talking," said Mr Saggamore.

Soon after we'd finished hoeing, Mr Saggamore told me one morning to take Boxer, one of the three horses, to the blacksmith to be shod.

"Get it done, afore we starts haymakin'. You know the way. Now look slippy, he'll be waiting for you."

I had to walk the horse about two and a half miles. It was a drippy morning, we'd had a shower of rain and it was still drizzling. The trees and hedges along the quiet lane were wet and dripping, birds perched there singing, glad of the moisture after the long dry spell. And on the roadside, thrushes tapped the shells of the snails that had ventured out.

The heat from the forge in the blacksmith's shop soon had Boxer steaming. "Proper fug in here," said the blacksmith. He placed one of the horse's forelegs on an iron tripod and began to bend back the nails on the upper side of the hoof. And then, having kicked the tripod aside, he placed the hoof, now bottom side up, between his leather apron covered knees and began to extract the nails holding the old shoe on with a large pair of pincers.

Just as he finished taking off the fourth shoe, Tom Prewett came in carrying two pieces of metal.

"Can you fix this for us, Ron?" he asked. "I allus thought it were a trumpery thing and yesterday it fell to flickets."

"Put it on the bench, and I'll have a look at it later on," said the blacksmith, who was trimming Boxer's hoofs with a curved knife.

"I ain't in no hurry," replied Mr Prewett, "I'll hang on, it's a wet morning."

"I shan't be able to see to it this morning, Tom."

"No matter, I'll bide yer a bit an' dry meself out by your fire."

The blacksmith began to heat strips of metal in the fire and I pumped the large handle which blew the bellows.

"Bear on," he said, and when the strips were white hot, he cut them into lengths on the anvil and then reheated them. Holding them with long tongs, he beat them into the shape of horse shoes on the anvil, with a hammer.

"That one old hoss, as your governor've got," he said between hammer blows, "don't half forever kick. The bugger'd kick a gnat's eye out."

The drizzling rain stopped and the sun shone through the dusty, grimy windows, lighting up the cobwebs which clung round the window frames. The blacksmith's tools were everywhere, hanging on the walls, on benches and on the floor. Across the roof beams were long bars of iron and steel. Smaller pieces littered the floor or were propped up in corners. Sheet metal leant against the wall by the forge. Shovels, spades, pitchforks stood against the opposite wall, many of these tools were worn, but they all had new handles with their owners' names chalked on them.

Bits of implements, newly repaired, lay on benches or on the floor. Outside were implements repaired, in the process of being repaired or awaiting repair.

Sparks fled from the metal on the anvil. The metal was re-heated, hammered and shaped, seven nail holes were punched in each shoe, the top centre clips were fashioned. The shoes were dipped in the tank of water near the fire and the water hissed and bubbled as clouds of steam arose. My arms ached from pumping the bellows. A punch was driven firmly into a shoe, and the blacksmith, holding the shoe by this, lifted up one of the horse's feet and tried the shoe for size. Clouds of acrid smoke arose from the horse's hoof. More pumping on the bellows, the shoes reheated, hammered and dipped. The smith clenched an upturned hoof between his knees, large-headed nails held in his mouth, and began to nail on a shoe.

"How's your governor going to pay?" he asked, hammering the last nail in, his mouth now free. "Thirty bob? Or a farthing for the first nail, a ha'penny for the second, a penny for the third, and so on?"

I told him that I had no idea which method Mr Saggamore would choose.

"He'd be a bloody fool if he chose the second. A farthin' the first and keep doublin' up, twenty-eight nails, it 'ud come to a tidy little sum. Set me up for the rest of my life, why, it'd be a bloody fortune."

"Eh up!" said the smith and quickly moved away from the horse who was straddling his hind legs. Urine gushed onto the floor, frothing and bubbling, it ran across the floor, dust floating on the surface. "Near like a flood," said the smith. "I'll be off now," said Prewett, going out through the doorway.

"Oh, I'd aim the pubs'll be open just now," said the smith, placing one of Boxer's feet on the tripod and tidying around his hoof with the rasp.

When I returned Mr Saggamore and Jack Musgrove were busy drilling turnips. "You need a wet back to drill turnips," said Mr Saggamore, laconically. He didn't mean a back wet from sweat; although I'm sure he would have considered that an advantage, to him sweat was a tangible sign of virtue; but that turnips should be sown in dabbledy weather. The swedes had been drilled three weeks previously. "But swedes are a chancy crop on this land," said Mr Saggamore after we'd drilled them, "as like as not they'll get the mildew and go rotten. Where I came from we could allus grow toppin' swedes."

I had seen and smelt fields of rotten swedes, the stink was something that was not easily forgotten.

The sheep are penned for dipping. Each one is caught and plunged into the submerged bath, and held under the dip by a pole fashioned for the purpose, only their heads above the grey liquid. The policeman stands by, stop watch in hand. Dipping is principally for the control of sheep scab, but it also controls the maggot fly, the ked and the sheep tick and louse. The dipping is compulsory and the policeman is there to see that it is done properly.

The sheep in the dip is released and it clambers up the stepped ramp at the opposite end of the bath, a swing gate is lifted and it joins the other sheep in the draining pen. It shakes its body vigorously, the dip flies in all directions and trickles back into the bath. Care has to be taken with the dip because it contains arsenic.

Once, Jack tells us, a quarrel broke out between a farmer and his workmen when dipping. The workmen threw the farmer into the sheep dip, the liquid got into his eyes and he couldn't see for a week or more.

Jack Musgrove began cutting the seeds when the red clover was out in boss (flower). This was the one-year ley (a mixture of ryegrass, red clover, trefoil and alsike), which had been sown under the barley the year before. Two cuts of hay would be taken and then it would be ploughed under and the field sown with wheat. Jack drove round and round the field in a clockwise direction (mowing machines have a "righthand cut") until the corners became sharp. I'hen he had to lift the cutting part of the machine and loop round back into his work. The clover and grass fell in heavy swaths, sometimes clinging to the swath board until it fell off in lumps. "Romboldy stuff," said Mr Saggamore, "but it's damn good fodder, and don't it throw up a crop. I'll warrant it'll cut nigh on two ton to the acre."

I began raking out for the back swath. "Keep the handle up," Mr Saggamore told me. Keeping the handle of the hayrake almost vertical prevented the teeth of the rake from digging into the ground.

Occasionally Jack had to stop to change the knife because a stone had broken one of the sections. Mr Saggamore brought repaired and sharpened knives out to the fields. "It's the small stones that break the sections, not the big stones. I put Bill to rolling this field in the spring and the muntle missed about as much as he rolled."

Next day Jack had almost finished mowing the clover. A small piece of the ley, the shape of the field in miniature, still remained standing. One end was pointed and had to be raked back for the machine. This meant I had to clear a way for the machine to leave and enter the standing crop. A quick flick with the rake and the swath was neatly turned over, cut stems uppermost in a continuous roll. The job was fascinating and oddly rewarding. When I had raked round the outside of the field I had, of course, been raking at the heads of the grasses.

Jack finished mowing. "I love the smell of new-mown hay," he said.

That evening I helped Reuben to erect a new stile by the church. Strictly speaking it wasn't a stile, but a squeeze-belly; two pieces of timber set close together in the ground, but curving outwards. The old one had gradually rotted away and Mr Winkleberry, the chairman of the parish council, had asked Reuben to put up a new one. He had stipulated that it must not be a climb-over stile but one which people would be able to squeeze through, hence its name, squeeze-belly. The footpath was used a lot and Reuben, no doubt with an eye on the generous proportions of some of the village women who used it, had allowed a similar generous gap between the two posts. Unfortunately the gap had been big enough to allow some heifers to get through as well. Mr Winkleberry, a fussy little man, told Reuben he must make the gap smaller. Reuben did so, and at the next parish council meeting, Mr Winkleberry and his fellow councillors had to contend with half-a-dozen irate fat women. Mr Winkleberry saw Reuben again and told him he must widen the gap.

So there we were, Reuben and I, puzzling over the size of the gap when Mr Bence came along. "You two look very perplexed," he said. We told him of our problem. "You see, Vicar," said Reuben, "it has to be small enough to stop a cow but big enough to allow a fat woman to pass through."

Mr Bence put on his pince-nez, which had been dangling on the end of a cord round his neck, and gazed at the posts thoughtfully. "Dear me," he said, after several minutes' contemplation, "A knotty problem. It would tax all the wisdom of Solomon. A knotty problem indeed."

"Mr Winkleberry's in a proper fidget about it," Reuben said glumly.

"I wish I could be of some assistance," said Mr Bence.

"I wish you could, Vicar," said Reuben hopefully.

"But I'm afraid the problem is quite beyond me." Mr Bence shook his head and his pince-nez dropped from his nose. "And I have a choir practice." He started walking towards the church, shaking his head and muttering, "A knotty problem, a knotty problem indeed."

Mrs Jenkins, wife of Fred who worked at Len Wilson's farm, was walking up the footpath towards us.

"Here's Fred's missus a-comin', her's a fair old dollop," said Reuben and added thoughtfully, "Her's not a bad sort of a 'ooman, I wonder?"

Mrs Jenkins was within nine or ten yards of us. "Hah," she said. "About time you oddsed that stile. I was wondering how I was going to get through. I come up this way to see my Mam, it ain't half a long way round the road. I said to Fred, I said, 'I'm goin' to take the short cut again tonight and if I can't get through I shall expect you to take an axe to that stile later on. It's not lawful, they ain't no right to block up a footpath. And I know my rights Fred Jenkins, it's your jooty to chop'n down.'"

"Well then," said Reuben, "if you don't mind helpin' for a few minutes, I think we can put it right for you."

"I don't mind sparin' a few minutes, if you'll put it right. This path's a big save," said Mrs Jenkins.

"Right then," said Reuben briskly and, grabbing his spade, "Stand right there in the gap, Missus, and we'll try'n for size."

I sat on the swathturner pulled by Boxer and started to turn the clover hay. The iron seat was patterned with the maker's name and Jack shouted, "You'll have Blackstone tattooed on your bum afore we've done with haymaking."

The machine turned two swaths at a time, I went in the same direction as the mowing machine. The two outside swaths I missed. Had I turned them, the backswath would have been thrown into the hedge. They would be turned last and in the opposite direction.

Old Caleb grumbled. "The boss ought never to let you turn that clover with that contraption, it'll knock all the goodness out of it. We never used to use contraptions, not to turn clover. Them big clover leaves be brittle, you'll knock 'em all off, you'll be losin' the best on't. We never used to use contraptions, we used to get out with 'ooden rakes, all in a line, one behind t'other. We didn't lose the broad leaves that way, but they don't care today, anything for quickness, anything for easiness. But it 'ouldn't a done in my young days.

* * *

A few mornings later, while milking, Mr Saggamore said, "Jack, when the sun's well up and the dew's off it, we'll start to walley up that clover and get some of it in." Jack grunted and went on with his milking. Caleb, who was just on his way to tip a bucket of milk into the container above the cooler, stopped and exclaimed, "You b'aint never aiming to rick that clover today, be you?"

Mr Saggamore said yes, that was his intention.

"But it ain't ever fit," expostulated Caleb.

"We'll put some salt with it," said Mr Saggamore, milking Bluebell, his favourite cow, quicker than usual.

"But it's gotta go in the bottom," said Caleb.

"We'll put some oat straw with it," replied Mr Saggamore, "and draw a sack up through it."

Caleb picked up his bucket of milk with an air of resignation. "It 'ould never a done in my young days," he sighed and took the milk into the dairy. He returned in a few minutes and sat down to another cow. "You'm askin' fer trouble, Boss," he muttered. "Thee casn't rick stuff like that without trouble."

Mr Saggamore finished milking Bluebell, emptied his bucket of milk and sat down to another cow.

"Whoa, whoa, my beauty," came from Caleb — his cow must have been fidgeting. "Whoa, whoa, my old beauty, steady, my old sweetheart," he said in the most soothing terms. "Now, now, my old sweetheart," in a gentle caressing voice. A scuffle. "Stand still, you old bugger!" shouted Caleb, his voice full of anger. "Or I'll byut the living daylights outa you!"

71

At about eleven o'clock, Jack helped me to fix extra tines on to the swathturner, which now became the siderake. "The boss is in a bit of a hurry," Jack told me. "He allus is. This clover could do with another day's sun on it. There's more hay spoilt in good weather than ever there is in bad. But it don't do to argue with him, he'll have his way whatever we chaps say, he allus do. It don't do to try and reason with him, it only makes him more ockerd."

"Will it heat and catch on fire?" I asked.

"It 'ould for anyone else but Mr Saggamore, he allus seems lucky.

Jack studied the sky for a few minutes. "It ain't goin' to rain," he said. "The wind's in the wrong place, and look how the cattle's walkin' about. That's a sure sign of fine weather."

Instead of turning the swaths the machine now flung two swaths into one, making a windrow, locally called a wally.

There was a reluctance in the men's approach to the starting of many farm operations. When Mr Saggamore proposed starting the spring cultivations, objections were raised, such as that the ground was too wet, and similar objections were raised when he said, "We'll start harrowing the wheat."

On the day the clover was cut they grumbled that it was too young, it wouldn't make, and now they said it was still too green to rick. Their objections did not stem from a reluctance to work, but from an innate cautiousness. And also, I felt, from the manner in which Mr Saggamore sprang it upon them. They liked jogging along, in a rut if you like. Had Mr Saggamore gradually attuned them to the idea there would, I think, have been less resistance from Jack at least. Though not from Caleb, Caleb appeared to object to everything which wasn't done in exactly the same manner as it had been done when he was a young man. He couldn't or wouldn't see any virtue in a method or machine which made work easier or quicker.

"If I didn't start carting hay," Mr Saggamore told me, "until my chaps said it was fit, it would be like rakings, the sun would have scorched most of the goodness out of it. It's all very well for old Jack to say there's more hay spoilt in good weather than bad, meaning getting the hay together too quickly while the weather's good. It can also mean if you don't get it quickly the sun'll scorch it all up. Nervous, all these farm chaps be nervous, frightened to get on with things and take a gamble. All farming's a gamble, that's why I can't understand those farmers who back horses, there's enough of a gamble in their job without going in for that damn fool business. A farmer came to see me one day to look at some of my bullocks and he said to me, "What's occupying your mind today?" And I said, "Why, my work of course." And he said, "No, no, I don't mean that." "What do you mean then?" I asked him. "Why, what horse are you interested in?" "I don't know as I'm more interested in one of my horses more than another," I said. "No, no. What horse have you got your money on today at the races?" I told him I didn't ever back horses and he was astounded. "Well, well. Fancy that. I've got to have a bit on every day to occupy my mind and give me a bit of an interest," he said.

"It's a damn fool of a game. Trying to get something for nothing, and it don't work, lad. The bookmakers are the only ones who make money out of that game. And they're the only ones who deserve to, they're the only ones who work."

The hay was dry and rustled when moved with a pike. If the decision to rick it had been left with me, I shouldn't have known what to do. I couldn't say then, and in fact it was several years before I knew for sure, when hay was fit to rick. Neither can I say when I did learn, I just knew. I did not learn consciously, like a child does at school, but rather I absorbed the knowledge unconsciously. Similarly with dozens of other things on a farm: when a cow would calve, or when oats were fit to cut. Or moving cattle into a fresh field.

In the summer Mr Saggamore would suddenly announce, "Those bullocks need a change of pasture." I didn't know why, there seemed ample grass in the meadow they were already in. In time I learnt these mysteries, and yet even now they remain mysteries in so far as I could not set down, in so many words, a rational explanation.

A wagon, complete with hay ladders (locally thripples, but as "thr" was invariably pronounced "dr", called dripples), was hitched behind the tractor and the hayloader hitched to the back of the wagon. Mr Saggamore grabbed a pike and jumped up into the front part of the wagon, while Jack clambered into the rear with his pike.

"Right, Bill, drive the tractor," ordered Mr Saggamore. Bill put the tractor in gear and shouted

"Hold tight!" Tractor, wagon and hayloader began to move forward, straddling the wally.

Bill lit a cigarette and put his right arm on the mudguard. "Watch that fag and look where you're going," shouted Mr Saggamore. The hayloader began to pick up the hay. Jack put a few pitchfuls under his feet and then began to pass the hay along to Mr Saggamore, who built the load. "Faster!" shouted Mr Saggamore once or twice. Once round the field and the load was well above the thripples. "Whoa!" shouted Mr Saggamore. "Hold tight!" shouted Bill and halted.

Bill took the rope which had been lodged on the tractor. He undid a short length of it and holding that end in one hand, flung the coil over the load with the other. Standing close to the load he called "Righto." "Righto," answered Mr Saggamore and Jack and then they slipped down the other side of the load, letting the rope slide through their hands.

Another wagon was hitched to the tractor and loader. This time Jack drove the tractor and Bill took his place on the rear of the wagon. When that wagon was loaded Bill went to help Caleb with the milking. When the third wagon was ready for loading, Jack said to me, "Right, young fella, jump up on the wagon and build the load. I'll show you how to do it. Let the boss drive and have a breather."

While we were starting Jack said, "One of them new chaps Rugman once had saw two of we chaps on the wagon, and in the pub afterwards he said to me, "You don't need two on the wagon. Where I come from one did that job." "Oh, you did, did you," I said. "Ah" he said, "I'll come along tomorrow night and put you in the way of it, if we ain't haymaking." "Very good on you," I said. And he came, and up he jumps on to the wagon, as sprack as you like. "I'll soon show you chaps," he said and shouts to Mr Saggamore, "Drive on." He hadn't gone far afore he was swamped with hay. "Hold on, hold on," he shouts, "I can't cope." Bill had to go and help him.

"When he comes down off the load, I says to him, 'I thought you could do it on your own.' 'Oh ah,' he says, 'but back home we went slow, there's no sense in going along at that rate.'"

The hay was coming on to the wagon thick and fast. Mr Saggamore had been gradually increasing the speed. Jack had no time to talk or I to listen, except for instructions. "Push it out further," he said. "Put plenty under your feet, don't let the hay get above you." No sooner had I moved one lot of hay than Jack had another pikeful waiting.

"The boss is allus like this, he don't half make you sweat on the load. Keeps pulling the throttle out a notch," said Jack.

Soon the load was well above the ladders. "Shout and tell him we're full up," yelled Jack. "Full up," I bellowed above the noise of the tractor, but Mr Saggamore drove on. "He's allus like this," said Jack, pushing hay towards me; clover leaves clung to the sweat on his face.

"I haven't room for any more," I said. "What shall I do with it?"

"Do what we allus gotta do," replied Jack.

"Full up!" I bellowed at the top of my voice, and then to Jack, "What's that?"

"Bung it overboard. 'Im'll stop when 'im sees it falling off."

Eventually Mr Saggamore stopped. When we were down on the ground he said, "You chaps let a lot fall off."

We loaded the fourth and last wagon. This time I drove the tractor. "Be sure to shout 'Hold tight' before you start or stop, else we'll be taken by surprise and flung off the load," Jack warned me.

By the time we'd finished that load, Bill and Caleb had returned. Bill had a basket containing our tea. We sat down in the shade of the load and drank our tea and ate the thick slices of bread, spread with butter and plum jam. "We allus used to cock the hay," said Caleb.

"I used to, but this way's quicker and easier," said Mr Saggamore.

"It ain't better though," said Caleb.

"That's as may be," said Mr Saggamore.

"Our Grit'll come and give us a 'and tomorrer night, aye 'im 'ull," said Bill.

"Ah, that's right, Bill," said Mr Saggamore, "Get your brother Gritton to come along tomorrow, then we'll be able to work double handed."

We unloaded some wagons. Mr Saggamore sprinkled salt on the rick and Caleb spread some oat straw among the hay. We reloaded the wagons and then Mr Saggamore said, "That'll do for tonight, the hay's going back." The sun was low in the sky, another hour and it would be behind the hill, the hay was beginning to get heavy and to lose its crisp rustle.

The four loads were covered with wagon sheets which were tied to the hooks under the bed of the wagon. "But it ain't goin' to rain," said Mr Saggamore.

"It'll be fine for wiks," said Jack.

"We'll have some of the home meadow down in the morning, Jack," said Mr Saggamore.

"It's goin' to be a scorcher tomorrer," said Caleb, "judging by the way the sun's goin' down. I only hope my poor old fit 'ull be able to last out."

"Aye," said Bill, "our Grit'll come and give us a 'and termorrer, if I d' ask'n aye 'im 'ull."

"I thought I'd missed you," said Miss Lydia Putterill. "You are late finishing tonight. I've been looking out for you. I heard you out haymaking and I guessed you'd be late finishing. I've been out here at this gate on the look out for quite twenty minutes and I began to think I must have missed you."

One or other of the Putterill sisters often waylaid me on my way home to ask me to bring them something from Father's shop next day.

"We've had a real day of accidents today, and I've got quite a list for you." She handed me a piece of paper with the familiar green writing. "You won't forget it, will you?" she said, as I remounted my bicycle. "You'll be sure and not forget," she called out after me.

Next morning, Jack Musgrove started cutting the home meadow. When I took a sharpened knife out to him the sun was already strong. While he was changing the knives, he remarked, "It looks as if it's goin' to be a scorcher, just like Caleb said." I could see the Misses Putterill's place from where I stood. Miss Hannah was vigorously using a scythe in one of the poultry paddocks. "Watch her," said Jack, "and you'll see why you've got to keep taking new tools."

We both stood and watched, shielding our eyes from the glare of the sun with our hands. Miss Hannah moved her arms and the scythe forward with force. We could not see the blade of the scythe or the grass she was cutting, only her head, shoulders and arms, and the handle of the scythe. Back and forth went her arms and the scythe a few times, then a pause. We could see from the backward pull of her shoulders and arms that something was wrong. "She's driven the blade into the ground," explained Jack. The blade was released, backwards and forwards went the scythe, then again a pause and a struggle. "She don't keep the heel on the ground, and she don't swing, she chops," said Jack. "Then she drives the point into the ground and buckles the blade."

I watched another struggle. "Now you know why they do allus want new blades," said Jack, climbing on to the tractor. "Begod, if the boss saw us stood here wasting time, he'd play hell."

"He wants you and the tractor over at the rick in an hour."

We unloaded the wagons. "They're harder to undo after they've been standing overnight," Mr Saggamore told me as we worked together on the rick. "But I like to get all the wagons loaded up at night, the hay keeps safe then. And it gives us something to do. We can't get at the hay out in the field until the dew's off it."

Gritton Lugg, Bill's brother, came and helped us that evening and succeeding evenings and Saturday afternoons. He was short and hadn't the powerful physique of Bill. He had red hair and a large forehead and walked with quick, jerky strides, his head held high and his chin jutting pugnaciously. Quite unlike Bill, who walked with a slow lumbering shuffle and with head hanging down. And, quite unlike Bill's manner which was quiet and almost humble, Gritton was cocky, knowledgeable and aggressive. "Grit's the clever one of the fambly," Jack told me. "He can use the telephone."

We finished the clover field; the rick was topped up. "A nice bit of stuff for me old cows," said Caleb.

"That'll be a good bit of grub for me 'osses," said Bill.

"The bullocks will be able to do their eye good and their bellies on that," said Mr Saggamore.

Jack and I said nothing. By this time I knew as well as Jack which animals would eat the clover.

Every morning Mr Saggamore went round the sheep, keeping a constant look out for maggots. Often I would accompany him. The lambs, being unshorn, were more prone to maggots than the ewes. I learnt to recognise the tell-tale dirty marks on their backs, the lambs twisting and biting themselves like a dog with fleas. More difficult to spot were those who gave no such obvious indications, but Mr Saggamore had an unerring instinct. While his dog held the sheep tightly in a corner he would make a swift dive in and catch an afflicted animal.

The blow-flies laid their eggs on the sheep and, if unattended, the maggots would eat the unfortunate animal alive, working their way into its stomach. We always carried bottles of diluted Jeyes fluid with us.

Some of the fluid would be poured over that part of the animal infected with maggots and with the finger tips it would be rubbed, rubbed, rubbed. The maggots would come tumbling out, wriggling and squirming. Then if the animal's skin had already been broken by the maggots, Stockholm tar would be smeared over the injury. Mr Saggamore called it "Stockhollum tar".

We finished the home meadow, and the next and the next and the next. At last the haymaking was completed. My feet were sore and my hands were blistered. Mr Saggamore looked at the palms of my hands and said, "Never mind, you'll get hard, tough skin grow there, like this," showing me his large calloused hands.

CHAPTER
FIVE

"In the sweat of thy face . . ."

GENESIS

The uncut roadside verges had become rank and unkempt, fescues and cow parsley had shed their seed and were dry and brittle as straws. The fields were parched and hard, cracks began to appear. Pastures were brown and the kale had turned blue. The large leaves of mangolds and sugar beet drooped, flaccid in the heat of the sun.

Sunday afternoon in late July. The horses, nose to tail, stood under the shade of an oak tree in the meadow, idly flicking their tails. Sheep lay panting in the orchard and pigs wallowed in the mud of a pool.

The heat shimmered across the fields. The corn began to show signs of ripening; oats turned yellow, beans turned black, and the wheat and barley began to dip their heads. Quietness, the air was still, not even the corn whispered.

I stared at the ripening corn. One could take pride and pleasure in sleek, handsome livestock, but they could not satisfy the heart like a field of ripening corn. "The wheat is beautiful," wrote Richard Jefferies, "but human life is labour."

Next day we started cutting a roadway round the oats ready for the binder. With sickles and wooden crooks, Mr Saggamore, Jack and Bill cut the oats and left them in neat sheaves. Caleb and I followed behind and bound the sheaves. We took a handful of straw, passed it head first under the sheaf and pulling it tight, twisted the straw round the neck of the heads and tucked the loose end under the bond. The bound sheaves were placed tight by the hedge out of the way of the binder on its first passage round the field.

The binder had been dragged from its hibernation and stood outside the barns. Poultry used it as a perching ground and it was smothered with their droppings. "Drat those hens," said Mr Saggamore as we cleaned and oiled it. "I know a man who won't allow his wife to keep hens on the place. They make such a mess, scrattin' and peckin' at everything. You can't leave a bin open for a second but what they're in it."

Poultry were the perquisite of the farmer's wife. They were fed cheaply on tail corn, meal, and after harvest their houses were taken out to the stubble and they lived on the shed corn. This cost the farmer's wife nothing and the income was her pocket money. But, in most cases, she was expected to provide her children with clothes out of the money. The Saggamores had four young children; had they not had children perhaps Mr Saggamore would have forbidden his wife to keep poultry.

The binder in its working position was too wide to transport along the highway. Two auxiliary wheels enabled it to be pulled sideways. Once in the field the binder was "unpacked", that is, it was put in its working position.

The standing corn was cut by a reciprocating knife between a row of fingers, like the mowing machine, but the speed of the knife was slower. The revolving sails gathered the crop on to the knife and made it fall uniformly on the platform canvas after being cut. Two more endless canvases took the corn to the binder deck where it was formed into sheaves, bound and ejected, butt ends first.

The canvases were of different sizes, and there was a difference of opinion about which went where and which way round. Eventually they were fitted in their right positions and Jack mounted the tractor. Mr Saggamore sat on the high seat on the binder, to see that the sheaves were being tied and to adjust the machine from time to time.

Later, Caleb, Bill and I started stooking the sheaves, six sheaves to the stook. The binder travelled anti-clockwise, and we went in the opposite direction so that we picked the sheaves up with their heads uppermost. Rabbits began to run out of the standing corn. Caleb was too old to chase them, but Bill and I managed to catch half-a-dozen. This wasn't so difficult as it sounds because the rabbits were confused; seeing a strange field they didn't know where to run. Some scuttled under sheaves, then it was a simple matter to flop on a sheaf and catch the frightened rabbit underneath. When there were only a few square yards left standing, an old dog fox came out and swiftly ran away to the hedgerow.

The oats were not fully ripe and would remain stooked in the fields for a fortnight or more. "Oats in stook must hear the church bells ring for three Sundays." Of course these oats wouldn't have the benefit of church bells at all, not unless there was an invasion. And that danger, so real a few years ago, had receded. Now we saw notices painted on walls in our market town, "INVADE EUROPE NOW." We wondered if the slogan painters would also be the invaders, but doubted it.

We hoped the church bells wouldn't ring, but it didn't alter the sense of the old saying. Sheep on the other hand should never hear the bells ring for three consecutive Sundays, which meant that sheep should not stop in the same field for that length of time. My limited experience of sheep told me that that was highly unlikely, the sheep themselves would see to that.

Jack Musgrove had a fund of such sayings. Here are a few of them.

"May kittens never make good cats."
I never discovered why.
"He that buys, ought to have a hundred eyes."
"From Christmas to May, weak cattle decay."
"Half your corn and half your hay on Candlemas day."

These last two were related and as I was to learn, very true. Candlemas day, the second of February, was halfway through the winter feeding season, so unless half the feeds, corn and hay, were still in the barns or ricks, the outlook was grim. And Christmas to May was the hard time for cattle, especially if food was short.

Those that were poor at Christmas only got poorer in the following months. Mr Saggamore used to say that a beast well summered was half wintered, another variation on the same theme. In May came the grass, "Dr Green" as Jack called it.

"You can't depend on grass," said Mr Saggamore, "not real grass, where a beast can bite and bite again, until the first week in May."

Another of Jack's sayings was "A gallon of milk from the cow is worth two from the bucket." All the calves at Suttridge were reared on cows rather than fed from the bucket and they proved that this was true.

Mr Saggamore was anxious to cut the first field of wheat. If it were delayed any longer some of the corn would "shed" from the ear as it was being reaped and bound. It was a good milling variety, a white wheat called Holdfast; its only disadvantage was a tendency to sprout in the stook in a wet season. In the next field, and due to be cut immediately after, was a red variety, Squarehead Master.

What lovely names the wheat had: Holdfast, Squarehead Master — so reliable that it was said, "When in doubt, plant Squarehead Master" — Yeoman, Little Joss (introduced in 1905), Bersée, Generosity, Jubilgem, and April Bearded, which as its name implies was a spring wheat and bearded like barley.

The names of oats implied abundance and indeed Abundance was the name of one variety. Others were Ayr Bounty, Bountiful, Onward, Superb, Black Supreme and Yielder.

There were less varieties of barley. Chevalier and Plumage were two of them. Mr Saggamore grew a variety called Spratt Archer. But beans were only beans.

Wheat did not heat in the stack like oats so it could be carted after a few days in the stook and also while the dew was still on it, in fact the dew helped to prevent the wheat shedding. The beans had to stay in the field as long as the oats, but we carted them early in the morning when the pods were softened by dew and therefore less brittle and the beans less likely to shed.

The horses were used to draw the wagons because they were more convenient than the tractor. A word to the horse and he would move to the next lot of stooks — one or more either side of the wagon, while with the tractor one of the two pitchers had to climb on to the tractor and then he got behind with his pitching. Two pitchers, (if there were enough men) to a wagon, one either side, one push with the pitchfork to push the stook down, then two sheaves would be impaled in the pitchfork and pitched, head first, on to the wagon. Not anywhere on the wagon, but where the loadbuilder indicated. Throwing the sheaves up, like putting them up butts first, was considered bad workmanship. As like as not the offender would have the sheaves flung back at him.

I learnt to load the wagons: heads inward, butts projecting over the sides, laid in orderly rows, another layer inside the first, then the middle filled to bind them. Each succeeding layer, fore and aft, over the ladders, could be made to project a little more, thus enabling the load to be bigger without increasing the height unduly for the pitchers. The wagon was unloaded in the reverse order, in a simple and orderly way, only the novice always found himself always standing on the one to be picked up.

When the Dutch barn was almost full, Mr Saggamore built corn stacks outside. The area was marked out with a thatching peg at each corner, and a thick layer of straw was spread over this area. This was the staddle and prevented the corn from coming in contact with the bare earth Sheaves were placed in the middle, after the fashion of a large stook, others were put round them heads inwards and uppermost.

The stacks were oblong. "I asked an old stackbuilder why he always built 'em round, and he said, because they're easier, but I can't get on with round 'uns," said Mr Saggamore. The stack got higher and higher. Mr Saggamore worked backwards starting at the outside, round and round, working towards the middle, half a sheaf placed on half of the sheaf from the round before. My job was to take the sheaves from Jack, who pitched them up from the wagon, and hand them the right way round to Mr Saggamore.

"Look at Jack, he don't start off in a hell fire hurry in the morning, but he's goin' the same speed at nine o'clock at night. Bill's all hustle bustle first thing in the morning, but he's done right in by six o'clock."

My first harvest. I had been with Uncle George to help at Mr Clutterbuck's, but this was my first real harvest, and it left an indelible impression on me. I see it now through a golden haze of sunlight and corn. No doubt the passing years have given it an added lustre. I feel I have at least held hands with the old style of farming, though of course it wasn't altogether the old style, this was the transitional stage. Tractors rattling the life out of beautiful old horse wagons. Until a few years ago, before tractors came to the farms (and remember, as far as we were concerned that was only three or four years ago), all the harvest would have been done by muscle power, horses' and men's.

We thought we were modern, hitching tractors to horse wagons, horse rakes and horse binders. At this stage the tractor was only an iron horse, used for pulling implements. Power take-offs and hydraulics were yet to come. Only the threshing contractor made use of any other power of the tractor, a pulley wheel to drive the threshing drum.

I'm glad I experienced it. The work was hard, I returned home each evening dog tired, but it was a healthy, satisfying tiredness.

Between loads Mr Saggamore and Jack strolled round and round the stack. With heads cocked they examined it critically. Stepping back a few paces and screwing their eyes, they made sure that the stack was symmetrical. A slight bulge, a tendency to lean one way, was noted and would be remedied with the next load.

The ultimate disgrace was for the stack to bulge or slip so badly that props had to be used. Mistakes in farming were on view to everyone. A much propped stack would be noticed by all the neighbours. The owner of the stack and his men would be subjected to remarks such as, "I see your stack's still there, but it's got so many legs that I shouldn't wonder if it walked away in the night."

Saggamore went round the outside of the stack, hitting it with a broad shovel to knock all the butts in neat and tidy. This had to be done immediately; if left the stack would settle and be too tight to "knock in".

The stack got higher and higher, way up above the top of a full load. Jack's work got harder. As we worked up he changed his pitchfork for one with a longer handle. Now I had to stand right on the edge of the stack, waiting to take the sheaves from him; no longer could he pitch them a few yards inside the stack. And I had to be careful to put every sheaf in the right position for Mr Saggamore. If I didn't, or if I handed one to him the wrong way round or flung it on top of the one he was about to pick up, he muttered and gave me a reproving look.

The sides of the stack were not absolutely vertical but pitched out slightly. The winter rains would then fall from the thatch well clear of the bottom of the stack and would not seep into the corn. When we were almost up to the top of the ladder, Mr Saggamore shouted down to Jack, "Time to start drawing her in, ain't it, Jack?"

And Jack, down below, covered in sweat, straw and corn, answered, "I'd aim it is."

Mr Saggamore started to draw the sheaves in a little each time round. The butts of the sheaves were not flat and he was careful to place each sheaf with the short end of the butt uppermost. Between loads he went down to the ground to make sure the roof was shaping properly. "We don't want her skew-wiff."

While Mr Saggamore and Jack were examining the stack, I remained on top. There was a good view, I could see Bill and the two Irishmen, Mick and Johnny, loading corn out in the field. They lived in a hostel with other Irishmen and came to England for work and money. In Ireland, they said, there was work, but too much for too little money. They sent money back home to their wives and children. Mick, it was rumoured, was in trouble, he had apparently been claiming for a non-existent wife, to escape payment of income tax.

Mick, tall, broad-shouldered, moved gracefully, rather like a cat; a fascinating, firm, square chin; handsome in a tough, rugged way. I saw him as an outdoor Hollywood hero. Johnny, smaller and gentle, would be deputy to Mick's sheriff. Or riding the range together, Mick the good bad man, Johnny his loyal friend. In the honky-tonk Western town, women would cluster and swoon round Mick, but they would confide in Johnny with his winning, shy smile and sympathetic manner. And this is exactly what the landgirls did do, in the pub on Saturday night.

Old Mr Williams, who had been carter at Suttridge for many years, had come out of retirement to help with the harvest. He led the horses out to the harvest field with the empty wagons returning with the full loads. As he got near to the stack yard, I heard the thud of the horses' hooves on the hard ground and the rattle of chains, the creak of leather as the horse strained against its collar, the rumble and creak of the wagon wheels. And then, as they came through the cobbled gateway, the sound of his hobnailed boots, the horse's shoes and the crunch of the wagon wheels, the crackle and the rustle as the sides of the load brushed the gateposts.

From my vantage point on top of the stack, I saw neighbouring farmers gathering their corn. Not far away, in Tom Prewett's small harvest field, he and another man were throwing sheaves into a tumbril. They flung a few dozen sheaves in the cart, then ambled off with it; on their return, they positioned horse and cart and before loading any more unhooked the cider cask and slung on the horses' hames, and had a good drink and a chat before continuing with their leisurely harvesting.

The Putterill sisters were having a bonfire. Scarcely a day went by, winter or summer, without them having a bonfire. Caleb was driving the cows in to be milked; most of the cows were dry now and he did the milking on his own in the afternoons.

The ladder was no longer visible from the top of the stack. Mr Saggamore had to fumble with his foot to find it when he wished to descend, something I viewed with trepidation. I was stationed in a small hole in the sloping roof, and taking the sheaves from Jack I pitched them high above my head to Mr Saggamore. The ridge on which he worked trembled and when it became narrower he abandoned his pike and worked with his hands, kneeling to place the sheaves.

When the last sheaf was put in position, Jack went into the barn and returned with a small bundle of thatching pegs which he handed up to me on the prongs of his pitchfork. I pitched them up to Mr Saggamore who used them to peg down the top row of sheaves.

"There, my boy, that'll stop the wind blowing 'em off. Enough work putting 'em up once."

* * *

A slight fall of rain had halted the carrying of corn that morning. Mr Saggamore and I walked across the stubble. The rain had filled the hollow centres of the stubble and as we trod on them they bent over with a crackle and then shot back upright, releasing the moisture which sent up a spray of water, up our trouser legs and over our clothes and faces.

"Land," said Mr Saggamore, planting a foot down firmly, "land, is the honestest thing. If ever you come into money, my boy, put it into land," and he planted a foot down more firmly than ever, as if to emphasise the point. "You may make more money out of stocks and shares, and then again you may not, you may wake up one morning to find it all gone, but the land is always there. There's been bad times in farming, but that ain't the fault of the land. I had a friend who had all his money in stocks and shares, and every morning he read the *Financial Times*. If his shares were up, he was too excited to eat any breakfast, and if they were down he was too downcast to eat. Either way he didn't get any breakfast.

"Then he sold the lot and bought land and now he eats his breakfast every morning, like I do. 'You can walk on land, feel it and farm it,' he says."

Jack had worked at Suttridge for years, back in the days when a Mr Wilcox had farmed it. Wilcox had also been a hay dealer and Mr Williams took wagon loads of hay to the collieries in the Forest of Dean for the pit ponies.

This meant an early start and Mr Williams had to be at the farm before five in the morning to give the horses their feed before the journey.

In those days, Caleb used to rule the roost at Suttridge, but many of the old farmworkers were autocrats, even the farmers had to let them have their own way. Both Jack and Mr Williams told me that Mr Wilcox never crossed Caleb in his heyday. It didn't suit Caleb for Mr Williams to be on the farm earlier than he was in the morning, so he contrived to arrive ten minutes before Mr Williams each morning. Milking started at half-past five in the morning (in order to catch the milk train, this was in the days before the Milk Marketing Board), and Caleb spent the forty-five minutes waiting for Jack, leaning on the cowyard gate smoking his pipe.

As soon as he saw Jack he shouted, "Ah, there you be, I bin waiting for you to get the cows in."

At half-past two in the afternoon, Caleb started milking again, so that milking was finished long before the official "knocking off" time, and on winter afternoons he spent the intervening time grinding up slabs of cow cake. The hand grinder was positioned by the cake house window so that, while he worked, Caleb could see who came and went at the farmhouse. Mrs Wilcox was, apparently, a great entertainer and was known locally as the Duchess of Suttridge.

I was told that Caleb used to have his own tools and if he couldn't find them — the Wilcox boys used to hide them sometimes — or if anyone else used them, perhaps a new worker — Caleb would announce that he couldn't work without his tools and would stump off home. How he managed to get away with it remains a mystery.

Times had changed for Caleb, he couldn't play the same tricks with Mr Saggamore. Now he relied on an ingratiating manner to get his own way, but even that didn't always work. Mr Saggamore, Jack and Bill treated him with a good-natured tolerance. More recently another change had come to Caleb: he had, in his own words, "turned to God". With tears in his eyes and with an emotional, quavering voice he told us that he thanked the good Lord for showing him the light.

Jack's comment was usually a couple of grunts, while Bill goggled with wide-eyed amazement but remained silent. Undeterred, Caleb would continue with his peroration: "I've been a wicked old man, but, thank the Lord, I've repented in time." Often there would be more, much more, in the same vein, a few tears trickling down the old man's broken-veined face lending authenticity to his conversion. I found it embarrassing. Jack was unimpressed by the exhibition.

"Mr Wellington has shown me the light. Mr Wellington is a God fearing man. And he's been good to me, many's the time he's given me a little gift. It isn't everybody who's good to a poor old man. 'We'll meet in Heaven, Sir,' I tell him." Caleb paused and gazed into the sky for a minute before going on, "'Except ye be converted and become as little children, ye shall not enter into the kingdom of heaven.' There, Jack, it says that in the good book."

This must have been too much for Jack who asked, "You got your seat booked in heaven then, Caleb?"

Later, when Caleb had gone, Jack remarked, "Proper old bible puncher, ain't he. But I notice he don't get on with that old squit when the boss is about. It's wonderful what old Caleb'll do for a pound of tripe."

Every Wednesday morning, Harry Wellington could be seen trotting past Suttridge Farm in his highbacked pony trap. He sold pork pies, sausages and tripe. Though his commodities were now in short supply, he still went his familiar rounds, and if he hadn't always got a pie, sausages or tripe for each of his customers, he still had a smile, a cheery wave or time for a pleasant chat with them all. Cheerful, chirpy, birdlike, small of stature, he exuded bonhomie. Everyone liked him, and a chat with Harry, it was said, was as good as a tonic. His blue eyes, as bright and sharp as jewels, missed nothing. He knew what was growing in everybody's fields, where there were mushrooms growing, the best nuts or blackberries.

He wore a bright cap, invariably back to front, and a loud checked jacket, absurdly long, it reached his knees. His little legs were encased in brown breeches and shining black leggings. On Sundays he wore a sober black suit with narrow trousers because on Sundays he preached at chapel. I had never heard him preach, but those who had said his sermons were very cheerful and, according to Mrs Biggs, "as for Heaven, he makes it sound as if you can hardly wait to get there. I try to get Colonel to come with me to hear him, but Colonel's never gone that much on religion."

Harry Wellington only had one regret: he regretted that his Uncle John was no longer with us. Harry couldn't have a conversation without mentioning Uncle John. Until his death Uncle John had lived at Cutt Mill, and Harry was continually wondering what Uncle John would have thought. On hearing any news, Harry's first words were, "Whatever would Uncle John have said?" On being presented with some problem, "What would Uncle John have done?" If he heard or saw something of which he disapproved Harry said, "Uncle John would never have allowed that," or "Uncle John would have done something about that." Eventually Harry would sigh, "What a pity Uncle John isn't still with us."

According to Harry, if Uncle John had still been alive and at Cutt Mill, there wouldn't have been a shortage of pig meal. "If Uncle John was still at the Mill, there'd have been plenty of pig food. And good stuff too, Uncle John would never grind rubbish."

There were forty or fifty acres of ground on to Cutt Mill and on those acres Uncle John grew bumper crops of first-class corn to grind in his water mill. He also fattened prize cattle and pigs, and no wonder with all that corn he ground.

Today the water mill, like Uncle John, is gone. I remember being taken as a very small boy, by Uncle George, to see it being dismantled. (Uncle John would never have allowed that.) The large mill pond has been drained and grows heavy crops of mangolds — whatever would Uncle John have said?

An oldish man named Edgar Tibbles now has Cutt Mill. He came there after fighting in the First World War (can Uncle John have been gone so long?). Now his own son is away fighting in the present war and Mr Tibbles has a job to manage. He suffers with rheumatism, but is determined to struggle on and keep the farm going for his son when he returns. Colonel does his ploughing, planting and reaping and Mr Tibbles' friends help with the roots, the hay and the corn and fruit. For the remainder of the year Mr Tibbles' friends sit round his cider casks.

Occasionally he buys a couple of yearling bullocks from Mr Saggamore; he won't have heifers because he says they are a nuisance, breaking out when they're bulling. When Bill and I have driven the bullocks over to Cutt Mill, we join the throng round the casks, but not for long, because we are conscious of Mr Saggamore.

One wet morning Bill and I went to Willow Farm to get half a dozen Hereford cattle which Mr Saggamore had bought from Mr Clutterbuck. On arrival we are taken into the cider house and Mr Clutterbuck hands us the "Wealthy and Great" mug brimful of cider. Most farms make, or get a neighbour to make, cider, and it is the custom to offer cider to all local visitors. Only one mug is ever used, it is handed round, each person taking a drink and passing it on to the next. When he isn't busy Mr Clutterbuck loves to talk, usually about old times and the old style of farming. I hang on to every word and would stop all day listening to such talk, but Bill, aware of what Mr Saggamore will say if we are late returning, is anxious to make a move. "We'll 'ave to be gwain, Mr Clutterbuck, ay us 'ull. What's the time?"

Mr Clutterbuck slowly extracts a gold watch from his waistcoat pocket. Holding the watch in the palm of his right hand, he stares at the dial, a puzzled look on his face.

"What time do you mean?" he asks, "God's time, my time, or war time?"

Mr Clutterbuck is in a muddle about the hours of the day, he has refused to put his watch on two hours during the summer and he is at odds with everyone else. It has caused confusion with everybody who deals with him, though greater trouble to himself, but he won't admit it. He is a lovable man, but stubborn and won't concede defeat, the result being that he doesn't know where or when he is. So now we have to go through this catechism: God's time (Greenwich Mean Time), Clutterbuck's time (British Summer Time), or War Time (Double Summer Time). Even when that's settled nobody's much the wiser, everyone is so confused not knowing whether to add or subtract an hour to get the required time.

"Oh ah," said Bill, realising his mistake too late. "We'd better be on our way, aye us 'ad."

"We'll go and get the bullocks," said Mr Clutterbuck, secretly relieved, I thought, by not having to go any further into the question of time.

As we walked towards the yard with the bullocks, Mr Clutterbuck said, "I shouldn't be selling them, but I need the money. However, I shouldn't grumble, farming's paying again, but it's a pity it took another war to do it."

Reaping, stooking, carting and stacking corn. Resisting the impulse to rub out in the hands another ear of wheat, puffing the chaff away, and then chewing the hard grains. A habit easily acquired but upsetting to the stomach. Horses make attempts to steal from the stook.

Some wild mint grew in the bean field and crushed, by foot or wheel, it smelt strongly; a weed, but its scent was pleasant, refreshing. In one field there were thistles in some of the sheaves, which wasn't so pleasant. "Scotchmen", Jack called them.

Unpleasant too were the barley awns which got under our clothes, working inwards and difficult to remove. They irritated the skin and eyes, making them itch.

Welcome were the intervals for meals. Bait at half-past ten in the morning, time for a quick bite of bread and cheese and a swallow of sharp cider. An hour's break from one to two, more bread and cheese (farmworkers had an extra cheese allowance), and an onion. The breed, cheese and onion cut with a pocket knife, dexterously perched on the blade with the assistance of the thumb and popped into the mouth. Or bread and lumps of cold, fat, salty bacon. More cider or cold tea swigged from the bottle.

Time then to stretch our aching muscles, extract thistles from our hands. Time above all for talk. The farm men loved reminiscing about old times, wondering what had happened to such-and-such or remembering the time old so-and-so had said or done something or other. When Edwin cried, "Hurray, the rabbit's gone," or when old Syd had asked for "whisky, because beer makes me drunk." Arcane, private jokes which brought great gusts of laughter. Old jokes, which I suspected were repeated year after year, and were the better loved at each subsequent telling. Gradually I began to understand and appreciate the farmworkers' dry sense of humour, often earthy, vulgar, but never obscene.

The quieter moments of reflection, the memories of past harvests, crops, animals, and of hardships too.

"It is good," said old Mr Williams, "to be back with the hosses. I allus loved hosses, but I never could abide cows, their shit's too soft."

Ten minutes for tea time. Thick slices of bread and butter spread with jam, cake and bottles of tea provided by Mrs Saggamore. And back to work until dusk.

The grass and clover seeds sown under the barley in spring had grown luxuriously. Instead of stooking the barley sheaves behind the binder, we left them lying flat on the ground to enable the sun to dry the greenery in their butts. The second cut of the one-year ley was taken, a much thinner crop than the first. Less clover, and the sun dried the ryegrasses which shrivelled and shrank.

The day came when we could see the end of harvest in sight. Eventually only a part of a field remained to be gathered.

"We're getting it up into a corner," said Mr Saggamore. A pause and a thoughtful stare. "Another harvest almost over." Did I, I wonder, detect a wistful note in his voice?

Everybody determined to finish the harvest that day. Glad the work was almost done, and yet a trifle sorry too. Jack, Bill and I went out for the last load, the moon our lantern. Jack built the load, while Bill and I pitched. With the last remaining stooks, Jack filled "his middle in". Bill picked up the last sheaf and said, "That's the one we bin lookin' for."

CHAPTER
SIX

"How a score of ewes now?"

SHALLOW

All the farms had orchards of Blaisdon Red plum trees and most gardens had at least a tree or two. A tall, upright tree, immune from most diseases, on our land it grew with all the careless vigour of a weed. It was first discovered growing in the West Gloucestershire village of Blaisdon. Apart from that its origins remain a mystery, but are a constant source of discussion and argument in the public houses. The variety grows on its own stock and, as it suckers freely, it is comparatively easy to find young trees for planting.

The plum is reputed not to thrive outside West Gloucestershire. I do not know whether this is strictly true or whether it is only said in order to keep a good thing to ourselves; nevertheless it is only grown in quantity in West Gloucestershire. The plums are oval and claret red, making an excellent jam. The trees are heavy croppers, providing an abundance of fruit most years. Before the war it was often extremely difficult to sell all the plums in a glut year and in the orchards they fell to the ground and were eaten by cattle, sheep and pigs. The pigs scrunched the stones and swallowed them, but the cattle and sheep spat them out, leaving neat little heaps of stones in the orchards, or, in the case of milking cows, in the cowshed mangers.

The gardens produced more plums than the households could use and the plums lay on the ground rotting and imparting a faint aroma, reminiscent of wine, to the garden.

Since the outbreak of war no plums are wasted; every one is wanted, the price is controlled and their sale is directed by the authorities.

Plum picking coincides with the corn harvest and a lot of them are picked by miners from the Forest of Dean. They take their holidays at this time of year and it has become a tradition with many of them to go plum picking. It must be a change from working underground, picking plums on the tall ladders. The tallest trees have no terror for them, these men whose normal work is constant danger. Holding an empty puller (large picking basket) in one hand, they almost run up the ladders. Hooks are tied to the handles of the pullers so that they can be hooked on to a ladder rung, thus leaving both hands free for picking.

Trees and ladders sway in the wind, but. with only one foot on the ladder, the pickers still stretch out bodies and arms for the plums. There is an art in moving a long ladder, the hands have to catch hold of the right rungs and the balance has to be perfect. And the ladder has to be correctly placed against the tree, almost upright (to

103

take the weight), and in such a way that, should it fall, it would fall into the centre of the tree. Some of the boughs of the tall old trees are not very safe, the wood having become brittle and partly rotten; "daddecky" is our term for such wood.

The orchards become alive with strange voices and laughter (the Foresters' accent is broader than ours), and are littered with bits of paper and empty tobacco packets, and the air is permeated by the acrid smell of strong tobacco smoke. Most of the miners roll their own cigarettes, using black shag tobacco. They squat on their haunches at the foot of the ladders, deftly rolling cigarettes and talking. Their faces, hands and arms have the blue scars of coal dust. The Forest of Dean is an island, neither England nor Wales, but most indisputably the Forest of Dean, and the Foresters are proud, independent, insular people. Speaking among themselves they use the terms "thee", "thou" and "butty", their words tend to slur together — "theesnow" instead of "you know"; to a stranger their speech would be almost unintelligible. They are a close-knit community — should an outsider upset one Forester, he would soon find he had upset all Foresters.

The Forester has a background of mining; iron mining, ochre mining, coal mining and quarrying, stretching back for generations. And yet, never far from farming, many of them run sheep and pigs in the Forest, grazing and free mining rights being jealously guarded.

During plum picking some of the miners live on the job, as it were, sleeping in a tallet (hay loft) overnight, so that they may be able to make an early start in the morning. They are expert pickers, many of them picking fifteen hundredweights a day. A few can manage to pick a ton if the trees are laden and the picking is easy. But as I heard a disembodied voice from a treetop say, "If theese wanta pick a tona day old 'un, theese gotta work a day and a half to do't, old butt."

Their days have no afternoon, only morning and evening. This puzzled me until I realised it was due to the influence of the pits, morning and evening shifts. Climbing up and down the ladders and standing on the rungs all day is tiring work that calls for a stout pair of boots. The miners wore their pit boots which had metal toe caps.

When we weren't busy with the corn, we also picked plums. The plums were tipped from the pullers into wooden boxes which held seventy pounds of plums. The miners were paid by the box and so had more incentive than Jack and Bill, and yet I was amazed to see how quickly they could pick plums and how dexterously they moved their ladders and swung out, with foot and arm extended, to gather the fruit from a bough.

Mr Saggamore affected to despise fruit and fruit men, but I noticed how quickly his boxes were filled and the way he too ran up and down the ladder.

As for myself, I hated the job. I was slow in picking and my fear of heights made the work almost a nightmare. I didn't mind the first twenty rungs, but after that I dreaded it. This must have shown because Bill remarked, "I can see you don't mind how high you go, as long as you've got one foot on the ground." He was right. It wasn't so bad if I went up the ladder cautiously without looking down, but of course I did look down and had an almost uncontrollable urge to throw myself off the ladder. And if the tree and ladder swayed, no matter how little, my heart was in my mouth and the palms of my hands were wet with sweat.

I was glad when it was time to collect up the boxes of plums or when I had to take a load to the station. Seeing what a useless picker I was and perhaps seeing or sensing my fear, Mr Saggamore always gave me these jobs.

I didn't take the plums to our village station, but to a halt-cum-siding about a mile from Suttridge Farm. The porter who had manned the halt had been called up and it was now staffed by a rough-looking, swarthy woman named Mrs Tunney.

On first acquaintance she was an awesome, formidable woman. On top of her black unruly hair, she wore a porter's cap askew. She smoked, drank and swore and her authority had gone to her head. She could be officious, cantankerous, abusive and downright impossible. In time I grew to like her, for underneath that rough, tough exterior I learnt there was a heart of gold.

The first time I took a load of plums to the siding, she came towards me shaking her fist in a threatening manner: "You're too late, too damn bloody late. You'll have to take the buggers back. You're too damn bloody late I say. I can't have you bringing plums here just when you feel like it."

She began gesticulating wildly with both arms, forcefully shaking her head. "Look at that poor horse sweating, I've a mind to report you to the cruelty man."

I was close enough now to smell her beery breath."It won't do, it won't do. I say it damn bloody won't do."

"Mr Saggamore told me to give you this," I said, taking a quart bottle of cider from the wagon and handing it to her. "Thanks, kid. Saggy ain't a bad old sort, is he? That's your truck down there, the third from this end."

On one occasion a representative from the fruit factory was present and objected to the state of the empty railway wagon. "You can't put plums in there, it's dirty and dusty. Mrs Tunney should have seen that it was clean. Wait a minute while I get her to sweep it out." I watched him limp towards the weighbridge shed-cum-ticket office and heard screams of abuse come from the shed. Later Mrs Tunney, followed by the man, strode towards the railway truck clutching a broom.

I offered to sweep the truck out, but Mrs Tunney insisted on doing it herself. The man whispered, "Let her do it. It is her job." Glowering and muttering, Mrs Tunney climbed into the truck, exposing an expanse of very dark hairy leg, between knicker and stocking. Once inside the truck, she planted both feet wide apart and pushed her peaked cap to the back of her head, and, with the brush grasped militantly, surveyed the interior. "There," she said, "there's nothing the matter with the truck. Not a bit of dirt, not a speck of dust."

The man walked away.

"It's as clean as a new pin. The man's barmy. He oughta be in the harmy instead of here hordering me about." She started sweeping, vigorously, aggressively. "It was as clean as a new pin," she said. But she managed to raise a surprisingly large cloud of dust, which made her cough. The dust was so thick that I could hardly see her, but I could hear the broom banging the sides of the truck. Eventually she finished and clambered out. I watched for that bare bit of leg; I could scarcely believe that a feminine thigh could be so hairy.

"Here, kid," she said a day or two later, "I've had the high-ups from Paddington down here this morning. They went to the station and the General (nickname of the Station Master), was frit to death of them. So he brought them down here, 'cos he knew I'd be able to cope with them. I told them a thing or two."

I had no idea who the high-ups were, or if they had indeed come from Paddington, but by this time I knew that Mrs Tunney was quite capable of telling them "a thing or two" whoever they were.

On my way to and from the halt, I passed a solitary stonebuilt house known as the Raven, which had once been a public house. Mr Warbley, its present occupier, was usually leaning on the garden gate, or standing in the road. At one time he had been the owner of two or three farms and comparatively wealthy, but drink and indolence, it was said, had been his downfall. His wife had kept him from the drink and made him work, but when she died his collapse had been quick and total. Now he was a shaky old man, white-haired and completely colourless; he looked as if the life blood had been drained from him.

The most striking thing about Mr Warbley was his extraordinary gentleness, as with a soft voice, like a velvet whisper, he would accost a perfect stranger without any embarrassment and try to cajole cigarettes or money. Uncle George never passed without giving him a packet of cigarettes or a half-a-crown. Most people said Mr Warbley was a fool to himself and undeserving; perhaps he was, but now that it's too late I wish that I'd given him a few cigarettes or sixpences.

Mark Twain once remarked that as he grew older he was surprised how much his father knew. I began to feel the same way about my father. A year or so ago I'd thought him rather a vague, indecisive man, always ready to evade problems and take refuge behind a newspaper. But, looking back, I see that it was only the trifling problems, things of no consequence, that he evaded. A placid man, he preferred to hide behind a newspaper rather than argue with Mother about things that he considered unimportant, but on bigger issues he was quite adamant, and Mother, who would shout and argue on small things, never argued with him then.

I began to see how right Father had been to send me to Ernest Saggamore's farm. The crops grown at Suttridge were the best in the district. Ernest Saggamore had no pretensions to education, speech or gentility, but was often rough and vulgar; a hard man to bargain with and sometimes a difficult man to work with or for, he was recognised as a just man, and out of this and his good crops and animals he had earned respect.

Saggamore's care and cultivations were just that bit more thorough. He had the knowledge, instinct, ability, knack, call it what you will, to know how and when every job should be done. His men shared in the respect his crops engendered. They endured and forgot his tantrums because, above all, they knew he was able and willing to do himself any task he set them. More than once I'd heard him say to neighbouring or visiting farmers, "I've never yet asked a man to do something that I couldn't or wouldn't do myself."

Less successful farmers, eyeing his crops and stock, said that Saggamore was lucky. Maybe, but I was beginning to see that good luck came with good management. And yet the reverse was not always true. Mr Saggamore was scornful and disbelieving of the farmer who boasted that he never had anything go wrong. After being told some exaggerated tale, Mr Saggamore would say, "I shan't 'ave 'e."

The one-year ley on the barley stubble was thick and luxuriant, but it wouldn't do, Mr Saggamore told me, to let it go through the winter like that. As it was too late in the year to make it into hay, he decided to let the cows graze it. There was a danger in this — the young clover, especially if it was wet, could "blow" the animals. "Blowing" or, to give it its proper name, "bloat", is when the rumen becomes distended with gas and the affected animal has a "blown-up" appearance. In severe cases death may result.

The cows were only allowed on the ley when it was dry, a careful watch was kept on them and they were driven off it after a short period. For five days the cows grazed the ley without any untoward incident, but on the sixth day several were badly blown. Affected animals can be treated with a drench or in severe cases by puncturing the stomach to release the gas. Either remedy must be applied quickly.

We drove the cows into the cowshed. Those which were badly blown had a job to stagger along. Bluebell fell down outside the cowshed and Mr Saggamore drove a knife into her stomach, but she was dead in a matter of minutes. While Bill and I tied the other cows up in the shed, Mr Saggamore ran to telephone for the veterinary surgeon. While we were waiting for him to return, Bill and I looked at the dead cow. "Bluebell were 'is favourite cow," said Bill, "'im 'ad tears in 'is eyes, aye 'im did."

"Fools grow fat in September." Harvesting, plum picking, hauling manure and spreading it on the wheat stubble, thatching, ploughing, and hedge trimming, gave us little time or chance to grow fat.

When the plum picking and corn harvest were finished, Jack started thatching the corn stack. The best wheat straw had been carefully saved for this purpose. The other materials needed were pegs about two foot long, usually made of split hazel, and binder twine. A long ladder, of course, is needed, also a hand rake (Jack made this out of a piece of wood and six-inch nails) to comb the straw, and the back of it to drive the pegs home, and a pair of shears, and a tank containing water to wet the straw before use.

Thatching entails a lot of kneeling on ladder rungs and so Jack wore knee pads made of old sacks. A layer of straw is first placed along the eaves as wide as the arms can stretch, then another layer above and so on, each layer overlapping. The straw is packed tight against the ladder's side. Pegs are driven in some six inches from

111

the edge, and twine tied to the pegs to secure the thatch. The pegs are then driven in at an angle sufficient for their heads to slope downwards; this is because if they were driven in vertically, rain would seep down them into the stack.

The straw was laid ears uppermost, though in some parts of the country it was laid the other way round. With Jack's method the butts of the straw were exposed, while the other method left the ears exposed so that, Jack told me, birds looking for stray grains of wheat left in the straw would damage the thatch.

It was usual to try and get most of the hedge trimming done during September, while the wood was still green and easily cut. Quick upward strokes of the hedge-bill left the sides with neat clean cuts. The tops were cut down tight to keep the hedge firm and level. A lightly-cut hedge top allowed the hedge to become "springy" and difficult to cut in succeeding years. Also, of course, the higher a hedge grew the harder the work became, making a man reach up to his work. Something a little under shoulder height was the optimum level for easy cutting and for a stockproof hedge. Swift strokes and a sharp hedge-bill were the secret of successful hedge trimming.

At Bannut Tree Farm, Fred Bloxham ignored the elementary rules of hedge trimming. His downward blows at the sides left the hedges jagged and untidy, while the tops resembled the switch-backs at a fair, where he skimmed over the tough places and cut the weaker places hard.

Dung hauling was Bill's favourite job. We loaded the manure into the horse-drawn dung carts and tipped it into small heaps on the wheat stubble, ready for spreading. The heaps were kept in straight rows and a few yards apart. The tailboard of the cart was removed and a quantity of dung was pulled out with a long-handled rake with four iron prongs. As the dung in the cart decreased, the cart was tipped a little higher. This tipping was a matter of heaving and balancing, and quickness too. If you weren't quick pushing the pin home, the load overbalanced and the lot slid out. Such a catastrophe was called a bishop. I have no idea why. We also called signposts bishops; formerly they had been called clergymen, because they pointed the way but didn't go themselves, but now that they had lost their signs and didn't even point the way, they became bishops.

Bill enjoyed the work. Like a lot of farmworkers he liked to settle into a routine. Also, he was the acknowledged master, for when it came to sheer hard work, there was none to equal Bill. I, too, came to enjoy the work, the smell of the manure mingling with the first tentative breath of autumn.

When all the field was covered with small heaps, we set about spreading them, using the small forks with four slightly curved prongs that we'd used for loading. As we flung the manure, a quick twist of the wrist ensured that it was evenly distributed. A few brushes with the back of the fork cleared the ground on which the heap had stood.

"There, there," said Caleb one day. "Only God would have thought of that. Nobody else would have thought of making a use for dung, and we'd have had it piled up everywhere."

* * *

The Ministry of Agriculture ran a series of advertisements in the newspapers giving advice to farmers. "Plough as early as you can. Between the stooks if necessary."

"I shan't 'ave 'e," said Mr Saggamore, scornfully. "Come a wet time, you'd 'ave a mess getting the corn away. And anyway, you'd be better employed carting the corn instead of fiddle-assing about ploughing between the stooks."

Another advertisement met with more response. "As soon as the corn is harvested, cultivate the stubbles lightly."

Cultivate was the operative word to Mr Saggamore, who never tired of saying, "An extra cultivation is better than a dressing of dung." The heavy cultivator was hitched to the tractor and dragged through a field of stubble. But Mr Saggamore wasn't a man to do things by halves; if light cultivation of stubble was beneficial, deep cultivation was bound to be more beneficial.

Light cultivation would stimulate the germination of weed seeds which would subsequently be ploughed in. But, reasoned Mr Saggamore, a deeper cultivation would also let air into the ground. However, when this particular stubble was ploughed the ground was wet, the tractor wheels couldn't get a grip in the loose soil, the stirred-up clods and roots clogged the plough. The furrows wouldn't turn over, the earth was not so much ploughing, but more like mooting by pigs. The frequent stops to unclog the plough drove Mr Saggamore into a rage. "Oh, why can't we get on like other people?" he roared.

The tractor wheels spun round and round, sending up showers of mud and straw, and little heaps of mud and stubble were left behind after the plough had been freed. And tightly packed mud, earth, straw and roots take some freeing from a plough. "Why can't we get on like other people?" asked Mr Saggamore in desperation. "That's the last time I ever listen to any Ministry advice."

This episode was one of the few times I ever experienced when Mr Saggamore's plans went awry. The work usually proceeded apace at Suttridge. On the rare occasions when it didn't, Saggamore usually flew into a rage. At such times everyone held their breath, even Jack, who was by no means frightened of him. Bill was though, he held Saggamore in awe and during Saggamore's tempers Bill gazed at him goggle-eyed and white-faced. But then, it was usually Bill who had to bear the brunt of it. The times I heard Bill say, "'im cussed and cussed and cussed I. But 'im was all right after, aye 'im was."

Saggamore's tempers scared me too. And old Caleb didn't make it any better by silently moving his lips, though I noticed he turned away from Saggamore to do it. I often wondered what those silent lips were mouthing. Was it a prayer, an incantation, or was he swearing back? It must have been something pretty fierce or powerful, as it caused great bubbles of froth to form at the corners of his mouth.

Every stoppage of work caused Saggamore to say, "Why can't we get on like other people?" Even the slightest hitch brought this question, and it was usually

115

asked in a voice of reproach. But we knew, and so did Mr Saggamore, that at Suttridge we got on much better and faster than other people. It wouldn't have been Saggamore's Suttridge if we hadn't.

However, even on the best run farms, times came when work was stopped. There was always the weather to contend with for one thing, and, sooner or later, breakages or the shortage or loss of some essential part of the equipment. I marvelled at the men's ingenuity, their gift of improvisation. "Oh well," Jack said on such occasions, "I suppose we'll have to make do and mend." And somehow they managed: large nuts used as washers to make a long bolt serve where a shorter one was needed, bent nails, wire used for all kinds of purposes. Wood, iron or tin fashioned into many shapes. Gate irons, leather straps and so on were put to uses their makers could scarcely have dreamed. Another hurdle desperately needed, a shaft broken at a crucial time — replacement or repair would be almost magically effected or repaired. Binder twine often played an important part in these improvisations and I never knew the time when the men couldn't produce a length of it from their pockets. Farmer's glory was their name for binder twine, a name justly earned.

When Jack had finished thatching, he began to plough the one-year ley in readiness for the wheat: first marking out the headland, about eight yards from the hedge all round the field, then setting up the tops.

I was given my first ploughing lesson on a piece of corn stubble, stubble being easier to plough than grassland. Mr Saggamore set up the tops and then stood on the footplate of the tractor while I drove, giving me instructions how to adjust the plough, how to straighten a kink in the furrow. At the headlands a lever was pulled which, by catching a ratchet in the ploughwheel, lifted the plough out of the ground. Afterwards he followed me for an hour or more, walking in the furrow, shouting instructions and waving his large hands in emphasis.

Ever since then I've preferred ploughing stubble. Not because I first ploughed stubble, nor because it's easier, but when ploughing grassland I have a slight tinge of remorse as the green sward is turned under; grass never looks so green and alive as when it's being ploughed.

Seagulls came in their hundreds, in search of worms which they tugged and stretched out of the upturned earth, their clamouring almost drowning the noise of the tractor. Fighting, flapping their wings and squawking, they swallowed the worms quickly, hungrily, greedily. They perched on the upturned furrows, in the empty furrows, or wheeled overhead, slashing the fresh earth with their white droppings.

Except at ploughing time the arrival of seagulls foretold bad weather:

> Seagull, seagull, stop on the sand,
> It's bad weather when you're on the land.

But they came in fine weather when the ploughs were at work; how they knew was a mystery.

Slowly up and down the field, the fresh-turned earth glistened moist and dark, gradually turning to a lighter shade after being exposed to the air for a while. The rasp or shriek of pebble and stone against the shining mouldboard, the occasional tantalising whiff of earth, while taking care that the furrows were neatly turned and of even depth and width. All grass and stubble had to be buried. The last strip between tops — emptying the furrow — had to be tidily done. No turning or driving over the ploughed land — that was an unpardonable crime. And in a few weeks' time all the neat work would be broken up by cultivators and harrows. There was sound utilitarian reason for good ploughing, but it was also done for aesthetic reasons, I'm sure.

During the spring, summer and early autumn Mr Greening was extremely busy, riding round the countryside on his bicycle gathering herbs, accompanied by his old sheepdog. We often saw this gnomelike little man with tanned face and alert brown eyes around Suttridge Farm, cutting and bundling up comfrey which grew by the stream and in some of the hedgerows and ditches.

Once, he told me, comfrey had been grown for pigs; little pigs fed on comfrey never scoured. Comfrey had the power to mend fractured bones, hence its old country name, Knitbone.

Mr Greening was a herbalist by profession. His father had been a farmer and a breeder of horses, but after serving in the army during the First World War, Mr Greening became a bookseller and then, later, a herbalist. From bookseller to herbalist, combined with a love of animals, was, he assured me, a natural step. He also made medicines for humans, but there was a handful of people who had a prejudice against this knowledgeable, likeable old man. This was not among the country people who often had great faith in herbal remedies, but among a few with pretensions to education. They called him a witch and his herbs they described as "dirty, filthy", using any method they could think of to denigrate this kindly old man.

Mr Greening was very talkative, eager to share his knowledge of herbs with those willing to listen. Pausing in his work he would light a cigarette, inhaling the smoke greedily and exclaiming, "It is good to smoke."

His knowledge of animals was as wide as his knowledge of plants. Just by looking at an animal he could tell its age exactly. I met him one day whilst ploughing and shared my flask of tea with him. His face was covered with scars and bruises. I asked if he had had an accident and was told that his house had been broken into and that he'd been set upon by hooligans. He was of the opinion that they'd been engaged to do this in order to drive him out of the little house he rented, and he feared they would return.

Couldn't he, I asked, move to somewhere safer? Mr Greening stopped tying up the bundles of large, prickly comfrey leaves and drew himself up very straight. "I was a soldier," he said, "and soldiers do not run away."

He tied the bundles of leaves on his bicycle and thanked me for the tea. "It is good to share," be said, as he mounted the bicycle and rode away slowly, followed by his dog. There was so much greenery strapped to the bicycle that I could scarcely see him.

* * *

The last Thursday in September was the day of the big sheep fair. Years ago it had also been a mop or hiring fair. Men and women looking for work went to the fair wearing a token of their trade: the shepherd had a tuft of wool in his hat, the cowman a tuft of hair from the cow's tail and the carter a whiplash. Women and girls seeking work as servants carried a mop. After bargaining about wages, the deal was sealed by a handshake and was binding for twelve months.

Almost every farmer for miles around attended this sheep sale. On this day, farmers of the Severn Vale met and mingled with the farmers of the Cotswold Hills. Some had sheep to sell, some wanted to buy sheep, others just went to have a day out. Fair day was one of the high days of the Gloucestershire farming year.

Mr Saggamore and I were sitting in the kitchen at Suttridge, waiting for Mr Saggamore senior and his son Henry. Mrs Saggamore was pouring each of us a cup of tea. She was plumpish, considerably younger than her husband, though one was surprised that she had such young children. Except in moments of excitement she was quiet and spoke very little, always looking at her husband, as if for approval, before making any definite statement. She habitually wore a worried expression. Unlike her husband, who with his energy seemed to grasp life eagerly with both hands, Mrs Saggamore, who certainly lacked his energy, appeared to find life a little bit too much for her. Despite their differing temperaments, they seemed a happily married couple, though I never heard Mrs Saggamore call him Ernest.

120

Mr Saggamore was reading the *Daily Mail*, his lips forming the words as he read. Mrs Saggamore pushed a cup of tea towards him. His cup, like mine, was only half full; she never filled a cup right full. He put the paper down and picked up the cup, and before drinking blew hard at the tea. Why, I don't know. Suttridge tea was never hot.

Mr Saggamore pointed the second finger of his right hand at me. "Look at that," he said. "See that scar there. When I was a boy I almost cut that finger right off with one of those old pop bottles. Just as I'd done it, an old man who was always chewing tobacco came to the backyard, "What have you done, boy?" he said and grabbed hold of my hand and spat a great wad of tobacco into the cut. Then he bound it up tightly and told me it would be all right. That tobacco didn't half give me gyp, but it saved my finger as you can see."

Mr Saggamore picked up his newspaper and resumed his laboured reading. A few minutes later he glanced at the clock on the high mantelshelf with a puzzled frown and said, "Where ever have they got to?"

The farmhouse at Suttridge, like most farmhouses in the locality, was sparsely furnished. The kitchen had an old-fashioned black iron range, which Mrs Saggamore said she hated, a plain deal table and half-a-dozen wooden chairs. Several large wooden cupboards lined the walls. Hanging from the walls were numerous calendars from auctioneers and merchants. The flag-stoned floor was bare except for a rag rug in front of the range. A pile of letters rested on the mantelshelf and behind the cheap alarm clock.

The dining room-cum-living room had a good oak table and sideboard, but the sofa and easy chairs were old and shabby, with stuffing peeping from them. A large overmantle with many mirrors was fixed over the fireplace. Several large framed prints hung on long cords from the picture rails; they were crinkled and stained by damp. There was also one oil painting, so dark and gloomy that I was unable to see what it depicted, but on several occasions Mr Saggamore had assured me that it was a beautiful picture.

Mr Saggamore drank his tea and when Mrs Saggamore had poured some more, he asked her to fetch his cheque book from upstairs. This morning Mr Saggamore smelt strongly of shaving soap and obviously he'd cut himself when shaving as he had several pieces of cotton wool stuck on his face.

Mrs Saggamore returned with his cheque book. "Where's Father and Henry?" he asked. "Just like our Henry, always late. I'll bet Father's in a state. But you can't shift Henry, he always was slow. When we was young Father always used to say that I could jump over Henry."

Eventually they arrived. Mr Saggamore senior was a short stocky man, wearing a bowler hat set square on his round head. He wore an old-fashioned jacket with tails, and narrow trousers. I knew him to be eighty-five years of age, but looking at him this morning it was difficult to believe him to be more than sixty-five.

Henry was, and looked, several years older than Ernest. His face was heavily lined and he was balding and running to fat. His movements were slow and deliberate and he appeared to be somewhat short of breath. Like Ernest he wore breeches, but his were narrow and dark brown, whilst Ernest's were light fawn, wide and smartly cut.

Henry and his father lived together. Old Mrs Saggamore had died years ago and Henry had never married. They ran the farm as a partnership, but it was obvious that old Mr Saggamore was the boss. I had the impression that Henry was extremely fond of his father but was entirely ruled by him. I could not imagine anyone ruling Ernest, but then Ernest was very different from Henry.

We got into Ernest Saggamore's car, Henry sitting in the front beside his brother, their father and me in the back. Old Mr Saggamore sat bolt upright, his walking stick clenched between his knees and his hands clasped over its handle. Mrs Saggamore stood by the car saying goodbye, her hands covered with flour. "Don't be late back," she said in a plaintive voice as we drove off.

"Martha do worry, you know," said Ernest Saggamore.

"It's my one day out in the year," said old Mr Saggamore. "I don't get out much now. I haven't been to Gloucester since last Fair Day. Do you know, young man, I haven't missed a Barton Fair for over sixty-five years. There won't be many at the Fair today who can say that."

Soon the two brothers in front were deep in talk between themselves. The old gentleman nudged me and said, "When them two get together they'll talk a hoss's leg off."

The brothers were discussing dairy cows. Henry, like Ernest, referred to heifers as "hayfers". "I've never milked a cow in my life," said old Mr Saggamore proudly. "Sheep, that's what I love, always have done. Owned me first ewe when I was five year old. Never been without sheep since.

"Henry's got sixteen milking cows. I walk down through the shed and never look at 'em," the old gentleman told me.

The brothers were discussing animal foods; I heard the words carbohydrates and protein several times. So did old Mr Saggamore who turned to me and said in a mocking voice, "Poteen, poteen. Henry and young Ernest keep talking about poteen. Poteen. I've fed animals all my life and I've never had to bother my head about poteen. Give 'em plenty of good grub and you don't have to bother about poteen."

The brothers were now discussing the merits of different varieties of wheat. Old Mr Saggamore was silent for a while then he nudged me again. "Do you know what I caught our Henry doing the other day?" he asked.

I shook my head.

"Weighing each cow's hay. I told him he'd be weighing their dung next." Old Mr Saggamore chuckled to himself and then poked Ernest in the back with his stick and said, "Your ground's too heavy for sheep."

"I wish you wouldn't do that, Father. You'll be the cause of an accident," grumbled Ernest.

"Now, now, Ernest. We're having a day out, don't spoil it by being surly," replied the old gentleman, winking at me.

124

The car was parked close to the market. Ernest Saggamore gave the attendant a shilling tip, and when we were out of the attendant's hearing remarked, "It pays to keep in with these fellows." He stopped, and so did his father and brother, then he wagged a finger at me and said, "A tip to people like that, and lorry drivers, is allus money well spent."

"Ah, and a bottle of whisky for the bobby at Christmas," said old Mr Saggamore.

"You're right there, Father," said Ernest. "Allus keep in with the policeman."

We moved on a few paces. I couldn't help noticing again Mr Ernest's wide breeches. One day I would have a farm and wear breeches like that, I resolved.

Old Mr Saggamore stopped; we all stopped. It's a strange thing, but apparently farmers cannot converse and walk at the same time. "I've never felt better in me life," said the old gentleman. "I've never had a day's illness in me life, but today I feel real kind." Then with a puckish grin he added, "I've a mind to enjoy meself today, my boys."

Our short walk to the market was interrupted several times when we met other farmers. Greetings, pleasantries and news were exchanged. All the farmers had an air of festivity. Old Mr Saggamore was congratulated on his health and on each occasion he told them how "sprack" he felt and boasted that he hadn't missed a fair for over sixty-five years.

"And what," asked one grizzled old farmer, "are you going to do with Henry when the pubs are shut?" This must have been meant as a joke, as the dozen pubs surrounding the market would remain open all day today.

"I shall have a drop of whisky," old Mr Saggamore told the grizzled one.

When we reached the market, many of the pens under the trees — there were dozens of plane trees in the market — were already full of sheep, and lorries were arriving with still more.

"Devil of a lot of sheep here today," said Mr Henry. The tailboards of lorries were being lowered and sheep were being driven into the few vacant pens.

"Mind your backs there," shouted the lorry drivers and drovers, flicking and waving their sticks. "Stand back there." "Clear a way." "Hup, hup, hup." "Hoy, hoy, hoy."

I saw Owen Tishforth, our local haulier, his unshaven face red from the exertion of driving sheep past the groups of gossiping farmers. Hand bells were ringing to announce the start of the auctions. Clerks were rushing to and fro, clutching bunches of papers. Sheep were bleating, baa-ing, drovers were shouting and swearing.

I noticed old Mr Saggamore was no longer with us and told Mr Ernest who replied, "I expect he's met some of his old cronies, we shan't see him again until tonight."

A small, dirty, down-at-heel man accosted us. "Can you let me have sixpence to buy a cup of tea, guv'nor?" he asked, and sniffed loudly. Mr Henry gave him sixpence, but instead of thanking him for it, the dirty man whined, "I ain't had a bite to eat today, guv'nor" — this time addressing Mr Ernest — "can you spare me a few coppers for a bun?

"And I'll warrant you ain't earned a bite neither," said Mr Ernest, turning on his heel. The little man placed a finger to a nostril and blew his nose before wandering off, muttering and with shoulders hunched. "That fella's a damn waster," said Mr Ernest. "You were a fool to give him anything, Henry." Later in the day, I saw the same dirty man in a corner at the back of the market with half a dozen other disreputable looking men, playing pitch-and-toss with half-crowns.

We stopped and looked at some Suffolk rams.

"There's some good tups," said Ernest.

"Father's thinking about buying a Suffolk tup," said Mr Henry. "The one he's got has got very slow."

"I might buy one to cross with my ewes," said Mr Ernest. "But Suffolk ewes are too heavy, I like a lighter, more active ewe.

"Father wouldn't have anything but Suffolks," said Mr Henry.

Farmers were jumping into the sheep pens and examining the sheep's mouths. One hefty farmer with a thick neck and a large red face glanced up at the Saggamore brothers and announced, "Broken-mouthed, every one of 'em."

The Saggamore brothers seemed to know and be known by almost everybody. Every few yards someone called out, "Mornin' Ernest. Mornin', Henry."

Now and then they stopped for a chat. "Got anything in here today?" asked a wizened old man in a blue serge suit. "No," replied Ernest. "I've never asked an auctioneer to sell anything for me, I can do all my own selling. Of course I've got his ground ready for drilling wheat. "My chaps are breaktions. I ain't goin' to pay somebody to do something I can do just as well myself."

A large powerfully-built farmer asked Mr Ernest if he'd got his ground ready for drilling wheat. "My chaps are breaking it down now," replied Mr Ernest, "but I never reckon to start planting before the second week in October." After he'd gone Mr Ernest said, "That was Roger Warren, a damn good farmer but wild as a March hare. Out hunting he'd jump anything, got a heart like a lion. A hasty-tempered fellow, up with his fists in a moment; when he's got the drink in him, it's look up."

We met Hesketh Newman, a frequent visitor to Suttridge. Mr Newman, as usual, was wearing a bowler hat, rakishly tilted, a spotted blue bow tie, mauve shirt, a long hunting-style jacket, breeches and high-legged boots. His mannerisms were exaggerated, slightly theatrical. His speech — he was a skilled raconteur — was verbose and flowery. He combined farming with cattle dealing and also wrote a weekly column for a newspaper. Until the war had put a stop to foxhunting, he had hunted regularly twice a week.

Another of his occupations was sketching. Anywhere, in the market, the farm or public house, he'd sketch people with a stubby pencil on a scrap of paper or even on a wall. The results were remarkably good, though he affected to belittle them, saying with a deprecating shrug, "Just a gift you know, but I'm afraid there's no talent there, but it amuses me — perhaps if I'd studied . . ."

Perhaps it would be apposite here to say a word about cattle dealers. There were two kinds of dealers, the rather shady kind, out to make a quick, easy profit and not too particular how they did it, and the reputable ones who provided a real service to farmers, buying and selling sound animals and content with a reasonable profit. Such a trade was skilled, the dealers had to be good judges of animals and know an animal's worth almost to a penny. They had to know where they could buy and where they could sell and know if the market was likely to rise or fall. Above all they had to be honest.

Several farmers, thinking dealing was an easy way to make money, had embarked upon the trade and ended up losing a considerable amount of money.

"See that man over there," said Mr Ernest, tugging at my arm and pointing towards a man with a purple blotchy face. "He's gambled and drunk a fortune away. Had one of the best farms in the district and now he's glad to make a living selling cattle medicines. C'mon quick, before he spots us and tries to get me to buy something."

Other farmers were pointed out to me. The rather non-descript little man in the shabby blue suit was, I was told, the best farmer in Gloucestershire. The big man with the thumbstick was the best sheep man in the county. The natty man with the malacca cane owed £100 to Mr Saggamore, though he doubted if he'd ever see it.

Several auctioneers were selling sheep simultaneously. In various parts of the market they stood on platforms between the rows of sheep pens, accompanied by a clerk with pencil and pad, and flanked on either side by farmers. We stopped and watched an auctioneer wearing a grey bowler hat and canary yellow waistcoat. He was much quieter than some of the other auctioneers, "How much am I bid, how much am I bid, how much am I bid?" he intoned, and then noticing the Saggamore brothers, he shouted, "Morning Henry, morning Ernest," and resumed his selling.

"Devil of a lot of sheep here," said Henry as we moved away.

"I could do with a score or two of ewes," said Ernest. "But this ain't the place to buy 'em. I think I'll slip up to the sale at Craven Arms next week."

I left the Saggamore brothers and went on an errand in the town for Mrs Saggamore. Afterwards I wandered round the streets surrounding the market. The public houses were packed, farmers even stood outside with glasses in their hands. The little shop that sold ropes, halters, muzzles, hay nets, rabbit nets and snares was doing a brisk business. So were the ironmonger, the barber, the tobacconist and the corn merchant.

I stopped and spoke to the garage man. "They say they're going to move the market after the war," he said. "I hope not, it's been my livelihood and my father's before me." Overhead I saw his name and the words, "Coachbuilders, Established 1895". "I hope they don't because nobody spends money like the farmer, when he's out."

The Saggamore brothers had told me I'd find them in the back room of the Wellington Hotel. Mr Newman was there, a glass of whisky in one hand, his other hand gesticulating as he spoke in his rapid, racy style. I also recognised in the haze of tobacco smoke Mr Stewart, the oil merchant. I liked this man and felt a tinge of regret for him now as I remembered him telling me, when he called at Suttridge one day, "I was studying to be a doctor, then my father died and I had to leave college and earn my living. When I hear a farmer's wife shout 'Here's the oil man,' I can't help thinking it might have been, 'Here's the doctor.'"

Mr Corrigan, the farmer who'd once ridden in the Grand National, had bushy sidewhiskers and was wearing a hunting stock and a tattered old jacket.

Mr Troy, manager of the town's largest agricultural machinery business, was a big, broad-shouldered, bespectacled man with incredibly small feet encased in highly polished brown shoes, who despite his bulk moved with agility on those small feet with a quickness and grace of a boxer or perhaps, though the simile seems ridiculous in connection with Mr Troy, a ballet dancer.

Mr Crackle, a corn and seed merchant, huge and ponderous, smoked a curved pipe, nodding and smiling sagely to all that was said, but saying nothing himself.

Mr Clifford, the cattle-food merchant, was short and stocky, almost as wide as he was high; his thick locks of hair curled round the back of his head and his ears, though the top of his head was bald, like a monk's. He was busy telling, in his staccato manner, a distinctly unmonklike story.

Mr Marshall, more genteel than most farmers, was tall, slim, slightly stooping, with an oval face and high forehead.

Mr Bennion, a Herefordshire farmer, much younger than the others, wore a brown pork pie hat thrust down hard on his large head, over his bushy eyebrows and red face and stood astride with his hands thrust deep in his breeches pockets.

Mr Clutterbuck stood by Henry Saggamore, just behind Ernest Saggamore and Mr Troy, both of whom were leaning on the counter talking. Over in the far corner slumped in a chair was Roger Warren, the wild, lion-hearted one.

Years later I learnt that these same men met here on most market days, forming a kind of club. Others might come and even try to join the circle, but receiving no encouragement they eventually drifted away, perhaps to join some other such gathering elsewhere.

"You haven't got much job to sell implements now, have you, Mr Troy?" asked Henry Saggamore.

Mr Troy turned sharply round to face him, "I could sell ten, twenty times the amount, Henry, if only I could get 'em," he answered. "If I took all the bribes that farmers offer me, I should be a rich man."

"Ah, times are good for farmers," said Mr Crackle.

"And for merchants," said Mr Bennion.

"Make the most of it," said Mr Clutterbuck dourly. "In my experience good times be short 'uns, it's the bad times that be long 'uns."

"It'll never be the same again," said Mr Bennion.

"Never is a long time," said Mr Clutterbuck.

"I can remember walking across a dozen wet, muddy fields to get an order for half a ton of cake," said Mr Clifford.

"Remember when Roger flung a full bottle of whisky in the fire?" asked Corrigan, sotto voce. "I'll bet there's times now when he could do with it."

"I remember when he flung a fox into the tap room of the Queen's Head," said Ernest Saggamore. And in a louder voice, "Hey, Roger, remember when you flung a fox into the Queen's Head?"

"I paid for all the bloody glasses and drink, didn't I?" growled Roger Warren.

Hesketh Newman started telling a story. The Saggamore brothers seemed in no hurry to leave. When at last we did leave the Wellington, Ernest parted from us to get his hair cut, promising to meet us in fifteen minutes in the teashop. I told Henry of the number of men waiting at the barber's shop. "Ernest won't be long," he said, and added, "Ernest always tips well."

Henry and I wandered round the market for a while before going to the teashop. After the clamour and hurly-burly of the market the teashop seemed sedate, demure, with its small polished oak tables, rush-seated chairs and vases of flowers. The woman behind the counter, who I assumed was the owner, was thin and middle-aged, and although she smiled, something about her made me think her to be a widow. She wore a loose fitting check gingham blouse which flowed out over her brown skirt; the blouse was cut low exposing veins around her neck, and the veins also showed prominently on the backs of her hands.

A telephone was ringing, but she made no move to answer it. A waitress, a girl of about sixteen also wearing a check gingham blouse, asked if she should answer the telephone, but was told, "Let it ring, let it ring, I know who it is."

The buns were stale but welcome, I'd had nothing to eat since breakfast.

"Tuck in," said Henry. "I'll order some more."

We talked about the sheep sale for a few minutes and then Henry began to talk about himself. "I wanted to be a carpenter, but Father wanted me to be a farmer. I didn't really mind, farming's got a hold on a farmer's son, but farming's changing, it's getting all rip and tear these days."

We ate our buns and drank our tea and fell into a companionable silence for a while. At length Henry said, with a wistful look on his wrinkled face, "I've always been one to lead a quiet life, I've never been one for going out much. I've always been a bit reserved, kept myself to myself, if you know what I mean. I know a devil of a lot of people, but I haven't any real friends."

Henry stirred his tea and looked pensive. "Shyness, that's my trouble. When I was young I was too shy to start courting and the years slipped by. It's too late now," he said ruefully. "I see my mistake now. When Father's gone I'll have nobody. Now, you just listen to me, young man, in a few years' time you find a nice young woman and marry her. I'd give the world to have children of my own now."

Ernest Saggamore arrived and sat down clumsily, muttering, "Scott can lose 'em. By jove, Scott can lose 'em" — Scott being the name of the barber.

If the drink had made Henry maudlin, it had made Ernest slow and ponderous. He fumbled with his teacup and kept dropping his hat on the floor. "These buns are dry, Henry," he said. "But, by jove, Scott can lose 'em. I watched him and can't he handle a pair of scissors and them there clippers." The brothers looked rather awkward sitting at the small table, clad in their breeches, leggings and stout market boots.

We drank more tea, and Henry lapsed into silence, but Ernest made fatuous remarks to the young waitress and from time to time muttered, "Scott can lose 'em." Soon we were the only customers remaining in the teashop. The waitress rather pointedly started tipping chairs forward on to tables.

"What's the matter, young woman?" asked Ernest. "You're all of a fidget."

"I think they want to close the shop and are waiting for us to go," I said.

"You want us to go, is that it?" asked Ernest.

"Well, it is closing time, Sir," she replied hesitantly.

"Well, we don't mind," said Ernest jovially, "We've got to be on our way."

"We won't stop where we're not wanted," Henry said good-humouredly.

"Here," said Ernest handing the waitress three half-crowns, "you can keep the change."

"Now," said Henry when we were in the street, "we've got to start looking for Father."

"We've got this performance every year," said Ernest to me.

"A devil of a performance it is too," said Henry. "Where shall we start?"

"The Spread Eagle," answered Ernest, clapping his hands together and rubbing them, a thing I'd seen him do many times when he was about to start a job, but then he always spat on his hands before catching hold of the tool he was about to use.

"The Spread Eagle," echoed Henry.

"We'll go through the market," said Ernest, "and see if we can see him."

There were several lorries being loaded with sheep in the market. We saw Owen Tishforth putting a Suffolk ram in his lorry. "Have you seen Father, Owen?" asked Ernest.

"Not for two or three hours," replied Owen. "What do you think of this tup, eh? The best 'un in the Fair today, I reckon."

"He's a wonderful good tup, he'll throw some good stock," replied Ernest.

"Devil of a good fella," agreed Henry.

"Your Father bought him," announced Owen.

We went into the Spread Eagle, but old Mr Saggamore wasn't to be seen. "Is Father here?" asked Ernest Saggamore.

"We'll try the Lamb," said Ernest.

"The Lamb," agreed Henry.

Ernest poked his head round the door of the Lamb. "Anybody seen Father?" we heard him ask. "He ain't there," he told us, "we'll try the Crown."

We reached the doorway to the Crown. "I'll try in here and you try the door round the corner, Henry," said Ernest. The brothers almost collided on the corner, then stood looking at each other shaking their heads. "The Prince Albert," announced Ernest grimly. "The Prince Albert," echoed Henry. We went up the stone steps to the Prince Albert, but old Mr Saggamore wasn't there.

"Where the hangment can Father be?" asked Ernest when we were out in the street again, with a touch of asperity in his voice. "It's too bad of him, beggaring off like this."

We found him in the Gloucester Inn, sitting round a table with half-a-dozen other old men, most of whom had their gnarled hands clasped over walking sticks. All of their weather-beaten faces looked flushed, and though there were beads of moisture in the corners, their eyes were clear as crystals. Deep in conversation they did not notice us at first, then old Mr Saggamore looked up and exclaimed, "Ah, there you are, me boys, I was wondering where you'd got to. I'm glad you've come, I'm just going to have a tune on the piano."

Henry and Ernest sat down and motioned me to do the same. I thought of Mrs Saggamore waiting anxiously at Suttridge. Old Mr Saggamore seated himself at the piano, lifted the lid and ran his fingers up and down the keyboard. Henry and Ernest settled down more comfortably as their father began to play. Henry leant over to me and said, "Father's a devil of a good chap on the piano."

CHAPTER
SEVEN

"The year grows lean . . ."

F. W. HARVEY

"I hate sales," said Mr Saggamore. "There's so much waiting and hanging about."

Most farms in the district were Michaelmas farms, that is, they were let from the twenty-ninth of September, Michaelmas Day, and if a farm was sold it was usually at this time of year. Consequently most sales of a farm's live and dead stock — dead stock, a peculiar description, being wagons, implements and the like, inanimate stock — were also held at this time. Such sales were infrequent at these times, farms were handed from father to son. Few farmers retired, and those without sons were more reluctant to retire now. Having farmed through bad times, they saw no reason to retire now that farming was profitable.

Several times I thought that Mr Saggamore would have the car in the ditch and we narrowly avoided colliding with an oncoming car, all this owing to the fact that he would not keep his eyes on the road, being too busy looking over hedges at neighbours' fields.

"Nice piece of kale there," he said rounding a bend and almost hitting a man on a bicycle.

"Damn fool, all over the road," grumbled Mr Saggamore. "Some of these cyclists think they own the road. And the beggars have the road for nothing. I can't understand for the life of me why they don't put a tax on bikes."

He was craning his neck again to look over a hedge at a field of sugar beet. "Half on't has gone to seed. I ain't surprised, he put it in too early. Well, look there!" We were passing another field. "He've bin and planted wheat in there already. It'll get too forrard, it'll look lovely at Christmas and be as yellow as a guinea by March."

The farm we were going to had been sold privately. It was rumoured that a Mr Woodcock had paid six thousand pounds for it and the general opinion was that "he must have been mad in his head to have paid such a price".

"I could have bought this place for well under a thousand a few years back," said Mr Saggamore.

The farm lay a few hundred yards ahead of us. "We'll pull in here," said Mr Saggamore, driving the car into a gateway. "It's a devil of a job to know where to park. If you're not careful you get hemmed in and then can't get away. Some on 'em'll stop here all day."

We walked up the lane towards the farm. Rain was falling steadily. Mr Saggamore hunched his shoulders and pulled up his coat collar. "The store cattle ought to be reasonable; they never sell so well in wet weather, they'll come into the ring looking tucked up and miserable. There's some good cattle here, I saw 'em last week, but they've been on some lush grass and that and the rain and the excitement will upset 'em. They'll poop all over each other when they're herded together and won't look worth half the money."

Several people were hurrying towards the farm buildings.

"Look at 'em," said Mr Saggamore scornfully. "Some on 'em'll break their necks to get to a sale, and most on 'em ain't got any business here. Look at him!" Mr Saggamore pointed to a short dapper man wearing a green pork pie hat, spotless riding mac and yellow gloves. It was unusual to see a farmer wearing gloves.

"Look at him," said Mr Saggamore again, twisting his lips. "He ain't got the money to buy a calf."

The man looked prosperous enough to me, and I said so. "Don't you never be taken in by that," replied Mr Saggamore.

The horses were being sold when we arrived at the farmyard. Horses were always sold first, then milking cows, store cattle, sheep, pigs, wagons, implements, harness, tools and oddments, in that order.

In other districts there was a different order. In Herefordshire, I believe they started with wagons and implements. Sometimes, as at this sale, there were lots of surplus furniture.

The carter was trotting a cart horse up and down the yard. The auctioneer with the grey bowler and yellow waistcoat was standing on a stone mounting block and beside him stood a clerk with a sheaf of papers.

The horse shied at the bystanders, who, alarmed, moved back several paces. "Whoa! whoa! whoa!" they cried.

"Just a bit of spirit," said the auctioneer breezily. "He's a good worker in all gears."

The next horse to be sold was described in the catalogue: "Bonny, Mare, 4 years; quiet, has been in shafts." She didn't appear to be quiet, there was a wild look in her eyes and the carter had difficulty in controlling her. The catalogue didn't say how long she'd been in shafts or if the shafts had survived the ordeal.

"Here's a young mare with a bit of life in her," said the auctioneer jovially.

But no one bid very eagerly for the young mare with a bit of life in her. Bidding was much keener for the next horse, "Duke, gelding, 9 years", who was docile.

"They don't want spirited young 'osses today," explained Mr Saggamore. "There ain't the chaps about what can handle 'em. A quiet old hoss that a land girl can manage is the sort that's in demand."

I heard a man behind us say, "— and this hoss had been standing still in the field, all alone. I thought there was summat funny about 'im, so I goes out into the field and gives him a good slap on his backside and still he don't move. So I says, 'Giddy up, old 'oss,' and gives him a shove, and do you know what, he falls down wallop. He were as dead as a nit. He died standing up there, fancy that."

From the expression on Mr Saggamore's face, I half expected him to turn round and say, "I shan't 'ave 'e."

The Shorthorn cows and heifers, described in the catalogue as "deep milking", met a brisk trade. Until quite recently most of the milking cattle in our district had been Shorthorns. Mr Trenchard had been the only

141

farmer who had a herd comprised solely of Friesians, but now the distinctive black and white Friesians had begun to appear, in small numbers, on many of the neighbouring farms.

A small woman in a long raincoat and wellingtons bought a number of the Shorthorns. She was a stranger, and when she'd made her first purchase the auctioneer had to ask for her name.

"Mrs Harrison, Mrs Zipporah Harrison," she shouted in a cultured accent.

She did her bidding with aplomb, waving a folded catalogue high above her head, oblivious, or not caring, about the curiosity she was arousing. She stood hatless in the rain, intent on her bidding. Her long black hair was wet and bedraggled, hanging in coils about her shoulders. Occasionally the wind blew strands of it across her dark, sharp-featured face and she brushed it aside with an impatient gesture.

"Never bid against a woman," Mr Saggamore muttered to me. A new and unsuspected trait in Mr Saggamore, I thought, but surely this was carrying chivalry a bit too far. Mr Saggamore turned to me again "They'll keep on bidding and run the price up. They think, if it's worth it to him, it's worth it to me."

Time and again I heard the auctioneer shout, "Mrs Harrison," as he brought his fist down smack. Farmers shook their heads, many stopped bidding against her. "No Ma'am," said the auctioneer once, "I won't take your bid against yourself." Mrs Harrison was unperturbed by the ripple of laughter that followed this remark, she just tossed her head and swept the hair from her face.

142

Trade on the beef store cattle was not so brisk; the emphasis in farming was on arable crops and milk. The auctioneer tried to encourage bids. The mildest of his witticisms were greeted with laughter. The young cattle were frightened and bemused by the crowd of people, clouds of steam rose from their backs as they milled around the improvised sale ring, and without lifting their tails they shot jets of green, watery muck over themselves. One bullock flicked his tail, spattering some over the onlookers. "Ha, a dirty trick," said the auctioneer, as everyone except the victims laughed. "A grand bunch of cattle," said the auctioneer.

"Sold to Ernest Saggamore," said the auctioneer a few moments later. I hadn't been aware that Mr Saggamore had been bidding, although I'd been standing next to him.

Six Hereford cross Shorthorn heifers were driven into the ring. Quivering with fright, one of the heifers tried to jump out. "Ho! Ho!" "Steady!" "Hi-hup!" shouted the farmers, brandishing sticks and waving catalogues. "Steady there!"

"Don't shout and wave sticks at them," admonished the auctioneer. He had become the stern schoolmaster instead of the genial wit. "You'll make them worse. You should know better."

The farmers stopped waving and shouting and looked suitably chastened. "That's better," said the auctioneer and beamed round the ring. The animals quietened, though steam still rose from their backs and their quivering flanks, wet and dark from the rain.

"Now, who's going to start 'em off?" asked the auctioneer. "C'mon, c'mon, none of us want to stand out here in the rain any longer than necessary."

143

Tom Prewett bid a ridiculously low figure, puffed out his chest, smirked and looked very proud of himself. The auctioneer looked pained. "I've come to sell these cattle, not give 'em away," he said. "Now come along, gentlemen, who's going to put in a sensible bid?" He pushed his grey bowler to the back of his head and pointed to Mr Saggamore. "Now, Ernest, start 'em off."

Mr Saggamore called out a figure, someone else bid slightly higher. "How much am I bid, how much am I bid," chanted the auctioneer, repeating each bid. Eventually the animals were sold. "Knocked down to Ernest Saggamore," cried the auctioneer. "You've got a bargain there, Ernest m'lad."

I'd watched Mr Saggamore very closely this time and noticed that he bid by jerking his head slightly. It was done so quickly, his head moved a fraction of an inch, almost unobservable, but the auctioneer knew.

There was little interest in the sheep, which surprised me after the hustle and excitement of the sheep fair last week. But Mr Saggamore explained that not many in this district really wanted sheep now that so much of their land was ploughed, they preferred to keep milking cows on what pasture they had.

The wagons and machinery, and implements capable of being hitched behind a tractor, were in demand. Nobody wanted the horse ploughs.

The rain stopped, and while Mr Saggamore chatted to Mr Clutterbuck I watched the sale of tools and oddments. The auctioneer came to a coil of rope. "What am I bid, what am I bid? Who'll say five bob? Four bob? Four bob, four bob, hang your bleeding self, four bob,

144

four bob," he chanted, a broad smile on his rubicund face. "What am I bid, what am I bid, five bob, five bob, thank you. Six, six, six bob, seven, done, seven bob Mr Cordwell."

He now stood in front of a pile of rubbish; rusty iron, nuts and bolts, short lengths of chain, pieces of broken implements. He looked around him. "Where's Joe?" he demanded. "Where's Joe?" The crowd took up the cry, "Where's Joe? Where's Joe?" they shouted. "Where've you got to, Joe?"

"Joe!" yelled the auctioneer.

"Joe!" chorused the crowd.

"We can't start 'til Joe gets here," said the auctioneer.

"Joe!" everyone shouted again.

Joe was a noted buyer of rubbish at sales, his stackyard was littered with such purchases.

"He was here a minute ago," said Owen Tishforth.

"Here's Joe," called Mr Cordwell.

Joe, a fat man of sixty-odd, came lumbering towards us.

"Where've you bin to?" asked Owen Tishforth.

"Had to go an' have a run out," puffed Joe. "Devil of a job to find a place with all these women about."

"What'll you bid for this lot, Joe?" asked the auctioneer. Joe tugged at his large stiff moustache and studied the heap.

"Ah!" he said at length and wiped the sweat from his big red face. "Ah."

"Well, Joe?" enquired the auctioneer.

"Ah," said Joe, scratching the back of his fat neck. "Ah," as he stirred the heap with his foot.

"What do you think of it, Joe?" asked the auctioneer invitingly.

Joe pushed his cap to the back of his head and looked even harder at the heap.

"C'mon man, do you like the look of it or not?" The auctioneer sounded a little impatient.

"Ah," said Joe, scratching the top of his head. "Some on it'll come in right handy. There's some useful stuff there. I'll give you five bob for't."

"What!" said the auctioneer, "only five bob for useful stuff like that?"

"Oh, all right, I'll give ten bob."

"Done," said the auctioneer.

Nobody liked potato picking except the two landgirls who came to help, Kate from Bristol and Madge from Birmingham. Kate had been a hairdresser and Madge a typist, and now they lived in a Land Army hostel and worked cheerfully in Gloucestershire fields.

Mr Saggamore was ill at ease with them. "I don't like employing women," he told us, "it's a job to know what to put them at." Forgetting that these landgirls had shown that they could hoe, haymake, harvest and thresh. And, on occasion, catch rats. Farmers who employed landgirls as part of their staff spoke highly of them. With cows and calves they were often better than men.

"I don't like having women on the place," he said, stamping his foot. But potato picking was the very devil, and reluctantly he telephoned the hostel.

Bill ploughed out several rows of potatoes with the bouting plough and horses. Mr Saggamore gave us all a little lecture, telling us to be sure to pick up every potato.

Kate and Madge soon proved themselves better potato pickers than us. Mr Saggamore strove valiantly to keep up with the girls. Puffing his cheeks and bending his back, he hurried along the rows throwing potatoes into his bucket, tipping the bucketfuls of potatoes into the sacks stationed along the rows. Gradually he drew ahead of the girls, but in his haste he'd missed potatoes along his row and Kate drew attention to them. "Ooh, Mr Saggamore! What a lot of potatoes you've left behind!"

"You'll have to do better than that, Mr Saggamore," teased Madge.

For a minute I thought Mr Saggamore was going to explode. Nobody had ever dared to criticise him before. He stared at the girls, his lips drawn tight and thin, his hand clenched the bucket handle and his knuckles showed white. Then slowly his face relaxed and a diffident smile appeared and the hand holding the bucket slackened. He looked like a small boy caught doing some minor misdeed. "Well, I never thought I'd be overtaken by a couple of slips of girls," he said.

"Just be more careful in future," chuckled Madge, "because we'll be watching you."

Bill would shyly proffer his packet of Woodbines and if the girls accepted his cigarettes his rough old face would glow with pleasure. Hours later, he would say to Jack and me, "I offered 'em a fag and they had one, ay 'em did."

"There's nothing clever in giving fags away," was Jack's usual retort.

Despite the lewd jokes and tales about landgirls, and the antics of a few farmers like Len Wilson, most farmers and farmworkers treated the landgirls with the utmost respect. They avoided such farming topics as might cause offence or embarrassment to the girls. Or so they said. I think it was to avoid embarrassment to themselves; many of the older men were very narrow minded. The men were very careful not to swear in front of the girls. Bill once reproved me for saying "damn" in their presence.

We were glad when we had the potatoes safely stored in a shed, but we were sorry to see the landgirls go. "Of course," said Mr Saggamore, "picking up taters is more of a girl's job I suppose. They wouldn't be much good at real work."

The horse no longer ruled the farming day. The tractor, unlike the horse, did not tire. From early morning until dusk the tractor could plough and cultivate the land for winter wheat. And at mealtimes a relief driver took over. The farmer was able to take advantage of good weather and soil conditions.

Instead of the time-consuming feeding of horses, it was only a matter of minutes filling the fuel tank of a tractor. Two tanks, a small one for petrol and a large one for vaporising oil. Turn the petrol on, four pulls on the starting handle with the lever in the off position, then with the lever in the on position, one swift pull and, if you were lucky, the tractor roared into life and was ready for a day's work. Then you had to remember to switch over to oil when the tractor had warmed up.

The smell of the vaporising oil fumes became part of my life — and so did the taste of the vaporising oil.

148

When the fuel pipe and carburettor blocked, you undid nuts and blew.

"You can do more after tea with a tractor," said Mr Saggamore, "than you can do all day with horses."

And yet he still used horses to drill his corn.

But farmers still tended to look askance at some machines. Two or three farmers had milking machines installed, but the majority viewed the milking machine with suspicion. This year a combine harvester did some of the harvesting on the War Ag farm. We flocked to see it, the local paper published a picture of it, but it was regarded as a novelty. It would never be a success in our climate, the corn would be damp, and in a wet time the monster would get bogged down. We smiled and shook our heads and went back to the serious business of harvesting with binder, sheaf and wagon.

The widespread use of the tractor marked the beginning of a fundamental change in farming. The horse had bred its own replacements and its food was grown on the farm. In the years to come farming would come to rely more on the outside world, the manufacturer, the scientist; the bull would virtually disappear from the farm and be replaced by artificial insemination. We didn't know it then, but soon the old economies would be discarded and in less than a decade farming would enter the world of the accountant.

The newly planted wheat was a green haze in the fields when we started mangold pulling. The left hand encircled and grasped the leaves and pulled the mangold, a flick with the knife in the right hand severed the leaves and sent the mangold hurling with a thud on to the heap. We took a square sixteen rows wide and made a heap in the middle of it; the severed leaves were dropped in a neat circle round the heap and at the end of the day, the heap would be covered by the leaves as a protection from the frost. We fell into a steady rhythm: grasp, pull, flick, thud. The repetition became automatic and satisfying. To get into the swing of a job, that was the thing.

On frosty mornings the leaves were white and crisp, and the left hand became frozen, numb. The numbness wore off and the hand tingled with exhilaration. The mellow October sun shone on the yellow and orange heaps of mangolds. The sun, the turning leaves of the trees, the sky in the late afternoon; our day, our world, became mangold shaped and coloured. Even today I've only to hear the word October and in my mind's eye I see the vision of mangolds.

We were pulling mangolds one afternoon when Hesketh Newman came. Bowler hat worn rakishly, he stood looking at the heaps of mangolds, the mangolds still to be pulled. Smoking a cigarette in short quick puffs, his gaunt body quivering with nervous energy, he exclaimed, "Ernest! Such mangolds, such mangolds! Never have I seen such mangolds!"

Cigarette now held between two fingers, he pointed to the cornstacks around the buildings which were now caught and lit by the slanting rays of the sun. "All those stacks of corn! They talk of the crops of the olden days, but Ernest, Ernest, they could never compare with these."

With elaborate, exaggerated gestures he pointed and waved his arms about him. "Such magnificent crops, the bounty of the fields, of labour and skill and loving care. Never in all my life did I behold such crops. The old farmers grew some wonderful crops, but what I see before me today makes them pale into insignificance." He paused for breath and with trembling fingers lit another cigarette. "Ernest, my dear fellow. Ernest, my dear old friend, I do most heartily commend you."

The mangolds were loaded into dung carts and hauled to the stone barn, tipped and thrown through the narrow side doorway into a large, high pile. When the barn would hold no more they were tipped and clamped outside. The clamps, buries we called them, were covered with straw, hedge and grass trimmings. Large forks with bulbous-ended prongs were used for loading, thus preventing the mangolds from being pierced and caused to bleed. In later years, I've seen mangolds being loaded with pikes being stuck into them, which caused me to shudder.

The sugar beet was lifted by the plough — a hope more than a realisation. When we pulled the beet, the long tap roots were still firmly anchored in the ground. We pulled at the tenacious roots and sometimes they snapped, but often it seemed as if we would have to pull the very ground from beneath our feet.

The pulled beet were left in rows the length of the field and when all the beet was pulled we went along the rows with beet toppers, cleaning and topping the beet. Leaves and crown were cut off; unlike mangolds beet did not "bleed", nor were they so susceptible to frost. When the roots were cleared, the sheep were turned into the fields to eat the crowns and leaves.

We tied old sacks, apron-style, around ourselves, and scraped and chopped for hour after hour. Often there was a bitter wind blowing across the field and some days the sun never shone and we were enveloped in mist. The beet was cold and muddy, sometimes covered with hoar frost or coated with a thin layer of ice. Our hands were wet, cold and muddy and in numbed and muddy hands the choppers were dangerous tools. And standing ankle-deep in mud and slush, our feet became frozen.

I had begun to dislike the beet back in the summer, those hours of foot-weary horse-hoeing, those days of back-breaking hand-hoeing, the annoying way the little plants had of twisting their roots round each other. But now, I positively hated the beet. As we worked, we talked in a desultory way, but most of the time we worked in silence, doggedly chopping away at the beet, enduring the cold, the wind, the mist or rain and the mud as best we could. We gritted our teeth, scraped mud from our senseless hands and stamped our feet, and occasionally put down our toppers to thump our arms about our chests.

The previous evening we had had rain and during the night a frost. The rain had frozen on the beet forming a covering of slick ice round them. We told the time by the trains, as only Jack carried a watch. The morning seemed so long that I thought I'd missed seeing the eleven fifteen. "What's the time?" I asked. "Eleven," replied Bill, who could usually tell the time within a few minutes without benefit of watch or train. But this particular morning I was sure that he was wrong. Jack slowly straightened his back, and scraped the mud off his hands with his topper. He pulled the round Zube tin out of his pocket and extracted his watch from its nest of sheep's wool. "Five past eleven," he said, and put the watch back in his pocket. From another pocket he produced a packet of Star cigarettes and a box of matches. "It's times like this when a fag comes in handy," he said. "It takes things off a bit."

At a quarter past three Caleb went to milk the cows and half an hour later Bill followed him. Seagulls flew in formation, homeward bound. The sky was grey, streaked with orange, and as it darkened the wood pigeons began to fly into the wood. At last we laid down our toppers and stumbled home, over the rows of beet and leaves. There was a sharp tang in the air; that night there would be a frost and next morning the beet would be covered with a crisp white fur.

Ten Italian prisoners of war arrived to help with the beet. They came each morning in a lorry and nine of them went to the field, topping beet, while the tenth man cooked for them in a roughly fashioned kitchen. His first job every morning was gathering firewood and a careful watch was kept on him. No wood was sacred, thatching pegs, stakes, even stakes out of the hedges. We found it impossible to keep a watch on him all day and Mr Saggamore tried to reason and explain. "O.K., O.K., comprehend. Similar," said the cook, smiling and waving his arms. But the Italians were known to smile and say, "O.K., O.K., comprehend," as soon as you uttered one word to them. That day two large bundles of thatching pegs disappeared. Next day Mr Saggamore instructed Bill to get them a cartload of old wood.

The cook searched the fields, wood and orchard for food. Turnips, swedes, kale tops, even the loathsome beet sizzled in the pot. Little hard, red cider apples were peeled and eaten raw by the Italians, to our amazement and their obvious enjoyment.

All kinds of strange fungi were cooked. Fungi which we thought were poisonous — they even ate the fungi which grew on tree trunks. We tried to warn them. They beamed and waved their arms expansively. "O.K., O.K.," they said, "very good, very good," and continued to eat. We feared they'd poison themselves, but each morning the same men returned, cheerful as ever.

We marvelled at their desire to please, their cheerfulness. Prisoners, away from their homes and families, and yet still friendly and cheerful. It was difficult to believe that until recently these men and our countrymen had been fighting each other. How different the cold muddy beet field must be from their own sunny land. And yet, they laughed and sang as they chopped the beet. On days when heavy rain made work in the field impossible, they crowded into their improvised kitchen and sang. On rainy days opera came to Suttridge.

They knew little English and we knew still less Italian. We communicated by gesture. "O.K." seemed universally understood, but the Italians claimed to understand us when they didn't. They chanted, "Comprehend,

comprehend," and "Similar, similar." Always "Similar, similar."

"Français?" one of them asked me. This could have been a common language, but my French was very restricted. "Ouvrez la porte" had limited uses, nor did "La plume de ma tante" lead to greater understanding.

Strictly against regulations, Mr Saggamore gave them small sums of money and we gave them cigarettes and hair oil. "Grazie, grazie," they chorused. They in turn made us presents of rings they had made and gave willow baskets to Mrs Saggamore.

Even Caleb, who'd been scathing about "Ightalians," at last succumbed to their charm, so much so that one day he brought them some of his home-cured bacon. "Grazie, grazie," they said, and began to eat it raw.

"No, no," said Caleb, dismayed, "you cook it. Cook it. Understand?"

They smiled at him and continued to eat the raw bacon. "No, no. Cook it," said Caleb, making gestures. Broader smiles from the Italians. "Cook bacon. No eat raw," wailed Caleb in desperation.

"Similar, similar," smiled the Italians who weren't too busy chewing to answer.

"They don't understand," Caleb said to Bill and me.

"Ah, understand," called two or three of them. "O.K., O.K.," said three or four more.

"They ain't bad sort of chaps for furriners," said Caleb, "but they ain't got no idea with bacon. I shan't bring 'em no more."

* * *

The beet was hauled to the roadside and tipped. There it would remain until the permits arrived from the beet factory, and then it would be taken to the railway halt and loaded into trucks. The field was wet and soggy and the horses strained in the shafts of the tip carts. "Tractors would be useless on a job like this," said Mr Saggamore. "They'll never take the place of 'osses on a job like this."

The cartwheels made ruts and the ruts got deeper each day. The ruts filled with water and overnight the water froze. In the mornings the wheels broke the ice and a mixture of ice, water and mud gushed ahead of the wheels like tidal waves. We stumbled along leading the horses and their hooves sent showers of mud over us. I thought nostalgically of those warm days of the harvest, when wheels and hooves sent up litte flurries of dust. I remembered the heat of the sun on our backs, the shimmer of heat, the whisper of straw, but the memory seemed dreamlike, unreal.

I remembered the day that Mr Teakle had talked to me about boots. How heavy, stiff and uncomfortable the boots had looked hanging in the shop, how comfortable they'd proved in the hot harvest field and now in the wet, cold beet field.

My boots and trouser bottoms were caked in mud. I learnt to walk with legs apart to prevent the mud working up my trouser legs. "What a funny walk you have," a lady said to me years later. "And so would you have," I replied, "if you had learnt to walk in a muddy beet field."

When we took the first trolley load of beet to the railway halt Mrs Tunney was busy in her shed. She was sitting in front of the fire shelling chestnuts. The prickly shells lay thick on the floor, covering her feet. In a corner was a piano accordion.

"I'm busy right now," she said. "Your truck is the fifth one from the end. I'll be out later."

Jack and I forked the beet up into the high railway truck. Tom Prewett came to catch the eleven fifteen and stopped to examine our beet. "They do say, that the more the beet is wrinkled, the more sugar it contains," he said.

"Going into town, Tom?" asked Jack.

"Aye. Got a bit of business to see to," replied Tom with a knowing wink.

"That man's a fool," said Jack, when Tom Prewett had moved away. "Even his own brother Oliver said so, and Oliver's a fool. Oliver's in the army now. Afore the war, Oliver was always out of a job and he had a dose of kids. His missus had one every year and Oliver's father had to keep putting his hand in his pocket to help 'em out."

Jack put another dozen forkfuls of beet into the truck before continuing with his story. "The old chap got fed up with it and one day he said to Oliver, 'You want to stop filling your guts with beer at night and going home getting kids. You want to stop that job, there's nothing clever in getting kids, any fool can do that.' And Oliver said, 'Oh, I don't know about that, Father. You'd never find a bigger fool than our Tom, and he ain't got no kids.'"

We resumed our beet forking. I thought I heard music. The music became louder. "Jack, can you hear music?"

Jack stopped working and listened; he was a bit hard of hearing and the train was arriving. We clambered into the railway truck. The passenger train was stopped beside the platform, but we managed to look over the top of the coaches and saw Mrs Tunney striding up and down the platform with the accordion strapped to herself.

"Well, well, well," said Jack. "Whatever will the old biddy get up to next? If we ever told people some of the things we see and hear, they'd never believe us."

The permits were slow in coming and we were still loading beet at Christmas time, to the accompaniment of carols by Mrs Tunney.

Every week, except when we were very busy, Mr Saggamore went to market and the whole farm heaved a sigh of relief. For a few hours we were free from his eagle eye. Caleb was free to chase Bill for matches to light his pipe and could sit on a bin in the cowshed smoking his pipe and counting a wad of banknotes.

Bill could drop wisps of hay on the ground without the immediate fear of wrath. Mr Saggamore was hot on wisps of hay. If a wisp, less than a handful, was dropped from a pike and not picked up by the dropper, Mr Saggamore would bend down, pick it up and complain, "It takes a lot of work to make this in the summer and I ain't having it wasted in the winter, or there'll be hell-to-pop."

Bill could and did leave gates open, doors undone and the lids of bins open, thereby allowing Mrs Saggamore's hens to eat, stretch and mess in the bins. He could give his horses an extra bowl of oats or filch some clover hay for them without being discovered, or at least not immediately, and Bill never thought or worried beyond the immediate future.

Mrs Saggamore usually accompanied her husband on market days, to do her shopping. When she didn't go she took the opportunity to get Bill to chop her firewood or to clean out her poultry houses.

Jack and I breathed more freely, with no Saggamore breathing down our necks. Sometimes we found time to do repairs, time for which Mr Saggamore would never allow. Mind you, he expected these jobs to be done, but begrudged the time to do them. If we had the time, Jack and I went into the wood to cut hazel sticks for thatching pegs. If at thatching time there was a dearth of thatching pegs (pegs being so handy for so many uses), Mr Saggamore would lament, "I can't understand why you chaps don't cut some in the winter, on those days when you've got nothing to do." But he'd never willingly allow Jack to go and cut them; in Mr Saggamore's days there were always plenty of other things to do.

Or we'd indulge in one of Jack's other favourite pastimes, sharpening tools, axes, bill hooks and hedge bills, on the grinding stone, me turning the handle.

Occasionally Henry Saggamore would arrive and drive into market with his brother and on their return Henry would stop for tea. I had the impression that Mrs Saggamore tolerated Henry rather than welcomed him. Since the day of the sheep fair if Henry saw me he would chat for a while, and as I got to know him better I found that he had quite a dry sense of humour. I found him an agreeable companion, but despite his quiet humour I found something sorrowful about him; he reminded me of a large amicable dog who'd lost his bone.

CHAPTER
EIGHT

"Is all our company here?"

QUINCE

It was a cold sharp Monday morning in early December. During the night there had been a heavy frost, the hardest we'd had this season. As I walked across the fields from the cowshed to the bullock yards and barns my ears tingled in the thick frosty air. The close-cropped grass under foot was crisp and white and crunched as I walked over it, the earth was hard and unyielding. Daylight had scarcely broken; a few stars still glimmered in the grey sky. I could just see the tall elm trees in the hedgerow and, as I drew closer, I could see that they were festooned with hoarfrost and the hedge itself, now bare of leaf, was clogged with it. A blackbird, its orange beak brilliant against the white, flew out of the hedge causing a shower of glittering particles of frost.

Opening the gate I disturbed a finch, breakfasting on the holly berries. The heavy crop of rich red berries looked even brighter in this world of white. The gate slammed behind me with a heavy dull thud. The old gnarled oaks surrounding the buildings looked even tougher this morning, appearing to me to have braced

161

themselves for this touch of hard, winter weather. A moorhen slithered across the ice on the pool.

I walked past the yard where a dozen large bullocks stood patiently waiting to be fed and, as they turned their heads towards me, twin jets of steaming breath shot from their nostrils. Like dragons, I thought, as I walked towards the stone barn, the nails of my boots ringing on the cobbled path.

I lifted the large iron latch on the big door of the stone barn and the cold metal clung to my fingers. Then I propped the door wide open to provide more light as I worked, filling the hopper of the root pulper and then turning the handle to cut the orange-fleshed swedes into fragrant slices which fell into the basket below. When the large oval basket was full, I pulled it out and grasping its handles, went over and tipped the sliced swedes into the bullocks' troughs.

The bullocks were no longer patient, and as I tipped the basket they jostled me, so that I had to be quick to avoid being knocked down. I sliced and carried three more baskets of swedes to them and still they pushed against me and each other, though only making half-hearted attempts to eat the swedes, only pushing and nuzzling them with their broad pink noses, until I had tipped some buckets of ground corn into the troughs.

Next, I went into the Dutch barn and cut some hay, remembering as Jack had taught me, to keep the back of the hay knife against the stack to ensure a vertical cut. I have never found a warmer, more pleasant job on a cold winter's day than cutting hay. And as I cut the hay, I fancied I was releasing those sunny days of June.

If the handles of the hay knife were the warmest, pike handles were the coldest, I thought as I gripped the pike and carried the hay to the bullocks' racks. But that was before I started carrying buckets of water to the bullocks.

I broke the ice on the pool with a hefty stake and dipped the buckets in. The water was brown, the colour of beer, stained by the annual fall of oak and willow leaves. The water from the pool on the other side of the barn was darker and thick from the seeping of the cattle yard. I carried a bucket of water in each hand, my hands getting colder with each succeeding journey. Gloves would have kept my hands warm, but my pride stopped me from wearing them — I could imagine the comments of Jack and Bill.

The threshing machine stood in the driveway of the Dutch barn. At one end of it stood the straw tier and at the other end a yellow Fordson tractor, all lined up ready for work. I stood just outside the barn and could see Fred the threshing machine driver, Fred the thresher as everyone called him, limping up the field towards me, his right shoulder thrust forward and a canvas bag dangling from it.

As he came closer, I saw that he had his cap pulled down low over his eyes, its brass popper exposed. His mouth was pulled in a hard tight line until he noticed me and said in a rasping voice, "Marnin'" exposing brown teeth with many gaps. He hung his satchel on the gatepost; the top of a brown bottle protruded from one corner. "It's a sharp 'un this marnin'," he said and added the usual remark made by farmworkers on cold mornings about there being more running noses . . .

163

While Fred was busying himself filling the tractor with water, petrol and vaporising oil, Jack and Bill arrived. The three of us then fixed the wire netting, which Fred carried with the threshing drum, around the stack. We were unable to make much of a job of it, but the law says it must be done to prevent rats escaping. We fiddled with the netting for quite a while, though it was, and looked, quite ineffective, but at least we'd made a token gesture and hoped that, should an inspector call, the law would be satisfied.

"It 'oont do any bloody good," said Bill.

"Well, us can't do any better," Jack replied. "I know it's only a tack in a turd, but if it don't suit the War Ag, they'd better damn well do it themselves."

Threshing requires a team of nine or ten men and Mr Saggamore had been doing some recruiting to augment our numbers. Caleb could largely be discounted; at the beginning and end of the day he would be busy with the cows, and also he was becoming too decrepit to do a full hard day's work. Fred would only supervise the running of his tackle, threshing drivers never caught hold of a pike nor a sack of corn.

Fred's mate Frank came roaring up the field on his motorbike. Frank was the feeder, he took the loose sheaves from the bond cutter and fed them into the threshing drum. Frank was tall and thin and looked good-humouredly at Fred as the latter rasped, "Marnin' Frank. Where the bloody 'ell you bin? Yer missus lay on yer shirt?"

Frank did not reply, he just grinned pleasantly at Fred, who scowled in return.

Mr Saggamore came into the barn with the first of our recruits, little Toby Ferris. Toby was a diminutive man, shy and quiet, too timid almost to speak. When he did speak it was in a hoarse whisper and he blushed to the roots of his colourless hair. A soft down grew on his face and his blue eyes had the innocent and wondering look of a young child. Looking at him, it was difficult to guess his age; he could have been forty or even sixty. Toby made a precarious living selling firewood and hawking it round with his pony and trap. He supplemented this income by doing odd jobs, but because of his lack of strength and skill, the work was usually low-paid. His wife was a complete contrast: she was a large, hefty, manly-looking woman with a gruff voice and black hair on her upper lip and chin. They were indeed an incongruous couple. Yet Mrs Toby would have strangled anyone who harmed her inoffensive little husband.

Next came Walter, who worked at Mr Clutterbuck's farm. Walter was stocky, strong and robust. Like Jack, he was skilled, reliable, the very best type of countryman, the kind of worker who is the backbone of any farm.

And last of all came Uncle George. He stopped his blue van — he'd recently changed his car for this van — outside the stackyard. He opened the door and with some huffing and grunting squeezed himself out.

"Here, Walter," he shouted, "just give me a hand to get this here cask out and help me tram it." When this was done, Uncle George looked round the assembled company and said, "Well, my men, I've brought you some of my beautiful cider."

Mr Saggamore began to apportion the various tasks. Bill and Walter on the corn rick. Toby to carry away the cavings. He'd just told me to go on top of the threshing drum to cut the bonds, when Uncle George boomed, "I'll take charge of the sacks of corn, Ernest."

Mr Saggamore stared at him for a minute before replying, "I was going to put Jack at that iob, and you on the straw rick.

"Rajah rhubarb, Ernest my boy, thee casn't order me about like that. It chun't as tho' I be working for money."

"Well," said Mr Saggamore, "I don't know."

"Well, I do," said Uncle George firmly, "I'll see to the corn.

"You'll have your hands full," said Mr Saggamore. "You've got to wheel the corn right round to that shed. It's a lot of work."

"You couldn't have come to a better chap then," boomed Uncle George.

Fred's tractor had been running for some time and now he shouted, "Be you all fit?"

"Ah, fit be damned," snapped Mr Saggamore, "let's make a start or we'll have dinner time on us."

Walter took off his jacket, revealing brawny arms, a large belly under his waistcoat and, slung under his belly, a broad leather belt. Bill tied some string round the bottoms of his trousers. Walter climbed the ladder which creaked ominously. "You want to keep off the pudden, Walt," someone shouted.

I stood on the deck of the thresher in a little pit and faced Frank across the large opening which the sheaves would go down. Jack pulled out the throttle and the speed of the pulley wheels increased. Flap, flap, went the huge crossed belt between tractor and drum. The drum beneath me began to shake. Walter tossed a sheaf to my feet, I picked it up and cut the bond with the knife. The knife had a piece of string attached to it which went round my wrist. I handed the sheaf to Frank who fed it into the drum.

Walter flung more sheaves down, I cut the bonds and handed the sheaves to Frank. As we increased our pace the noise of the thresher settled down to a steady hum. In half an hour Walter had cleared enough space for Bill to join him on the bay of wheat. Walter needed help now, Bill throwing the sheaves forward to him.

A cold breeze began to blow through the barn. "Somebody ain't shut the gate," Frank shouted to me above the noise of the machinery.

Bill worked round and round the bay of wheat, picking up sheaves and passing them to Walter, who flung them down to me. I picked them up and slid the blade of the knife under the strings. A quick turn of the blade cut the string. Frank took the sheaves from my outstretched arms and fed them evenly into the drum. The monster seemed insatiable, and we its slaves. Down below attendant slaves dealt with its discharge. Uncle George took the full sacks of corn from the machine, tied them up and wheeled them away. Four bushel sacks contained two and a quarter hundred weights of wheat, leaving just enough room to gather the top of the sack, pleat it and tie the strings (which I had saved) with a slip knot so that the bag would be easy to untie when we came to weigh the corn.

167

The threshed straw came out from the top of the other end of the drum and tumbled into the bolten tier, which was driven by a chain from the drum. Mr Saggamore picked up the boltens and pitched them on to the stack Jack was building outside. When Caleb came, he took the bolters from the tier and flung them to Mr Saggamore, thereby lessening the distance Mr Saggamore had to carry them.

Jack plunged about on the straw stack, his feet sinking deeply into the straw. At mid-morning, old Mr Williams appeared, well muffled up. I saw him remove a jacket and later, when I looked round, he was on the straw stack helping Jack.

"Now we're all right, we've got a good team," I heard Mr Saggamore shout. "We shall be able to shift summat if the tack do hold."

With a root fork Toby removed the cavings from under the drum and, using a beet pulp sack cut open, carried them away. Toby had the dirtiest job; we were all covered in dust, but none so bad as Toby. Dust caked our clothes and faces and clung to our eyebrows, lodged on our eyelids and made them itch, clogged our eyes, got up our noses, down our necks and throats, but poor Toby was shrouded in dust.

Fred walked round the tackle with a spanner and an oil can, tightening nuts and squirting oil on bearings, or stood just outside the barn smoking a cigarette in the sunshine. Dust danced in the rays of the sun and the smoke from his cigarette wafted blue and tantalising into the barn. But mostly he stood by the cider cask, often joined by Uncle George.

Every so often Fred filled a stone jar with cider and brought it round to each of us in turn. The inside of the chipped old thick china cup was soon coated with dust. Fred carefully wiped it with an oily forefinger and then with the jar in the crook of his arm filled the cup, leaving an oily film floating on the top of the cider.

The cider washed the dust down our throats and the effect of repeated cups helped to dull the senses enough to enable us to put up with the work, the monotony, the dust and the cold, with equanimity.

Walter was down to the level of the thresher's deck. Occasionally he and I misjudged our timing, and as I bent down to pick up a sheaf, the hard sharp butt of another would hit my face. Occasionally too, I let an uncut sheaf fall into the thresher. "Whumph," went the monster and its guts rumbled. Frank would give me a rueful grin and Fred would look up, shout and shake his fist menacingly.

Fred and Uncle George spent much time at the cider cask. The morning seemed interminable, but at last Fred whistled and shouted, "Dinner time, clear the deck." I cut the sheaves and gathered the loose straw which had collected about my feet and then brushed the fallen grain into the drum, before descending the ladder. Fred stopped the tractor; the sudden quietness seemed unreal. Walter and Bill were already sitting on bolters of straw, their backs against the straw rick, when I reached the ground. Soon they were joined by Jack and Frank. All of them placed their "tommy-bags" in their laps and took food out of them: bread, cheese and onions.

"Fred's allus on, he wants to work Sundays an' all," said Frank as he peeled an onion. "But six days a wik is enough at this work. 'Sides, he ain't got a wife and kids and a large garden."

"Fred's married, en't he?" asked Jack.

"Not in church," Frank answered.

Fred, who'd been refilling the cider jar, now joined us. "Good bit of corn," he said, sitting down and placing the jar at his feet.

"It's nice sittin' here in the sun," said Frank, "better'n squat in front of a fire."

Uncle George brought an old box and sat beside us, observing, "If I sat down low like that, I doubt if I'd get up."

"Do you do Linley's dreshing, Fred?" asked Jack.

"No," growled Fred.

"Ah, I thought you didn't," said Jack. "You bain't posh enough to do 'is'n."

"'Im con 'ave who 'im likes, con't 'im?" asked Fred belligerently.

"Now, now, now," rumbled Uncle George, "don't argify. Have some of my nice cider instead."

"I gotta drop of cold tea in me tommy-bag, but I'll kip that fer later," said Fred, pulling viciously at a crust of bread with his teeth.

Bill handed cups of cider round and Uncle George looked benevolently at everyone. "There, there," he said in soothing tones, and chewing at a large wedge of cold fat bacon and bread, "Drink, drink. Drink for thy stomach's sake and don't yut to kill thyselves."

"'Ow's it going up at your place, Walt?" asked Jack.

"We'm a bit short 'anded. Clutterbuck's talkin' about 'avin' a landgirl to live in," said Walter.

"I remember doin' dreshin' wi' a flail," said old Mr Williams. "Stick an' a 'alf some called it. Thump, thump, thump, across the barn floor all day. It were back breakin' work, and you 'ad to 'ave the knack on't or you'd get a thump across the yud an' all."

"Corn's running well," said Uncle George. "It makes the sweat run out of me, wheeling it away on the sack truck."

"You still find time to give that cask a fair talkin' to," said Walter.

"What be you infusin'?" asked Uncle George.

"Oh, nothing, nothing," said Walter, with a wink at the rest of us.

"I'm glad of that, Walt. I shouldn't like to think that old Arthur Clutterbuck had a man laid up in hospital."

Our conversation was cut short by the return of Mr Saggamore. "C'mon my lads. It's time we made a start," he said.

"Dinner time ain't up yet," muttered Bill, who'd just lit another cigarette.

"Shut yer mouth, you fool," hissed Jack.

We all scrambled to our feet, as Fred went over to the tractor and caught hold of the starting handle. The men all moved to their working positions and Mr Saggamore spat on the palms of his hands and rubbed them together before grasping his pike handle.

Soon the bay of wheat was well below the deck of the thresher. "It's uphill work now," said Walter as he pitched the sheaves to me. The lower the bay of wheat got the dustier the work became, and the cider was even more welcome. Uncle George, who had the cleanest job, was seen more often at the cask, while full sacks, untied, remained near the thresher.

Rats began to appear. Bill and Walter managed to kill some with their pikes, but many escaped. At about three o'clock, a belt on the thresher broke and we had a respite while Fred mended it. A quarter of an hour later, Walter let out a dreadful howl, so loud and terrible that everyone heard it and turned to look at him. Walter stood still on the stack, his face white and strained, while his hands clasped his thigh, beads of sweat glistening on his brow. All work stopped as we stared at Walter. His hand moved slowly, furtively up his thigh and for another second or two we silently gaped as Walter desperately groped.

"I've got the bugger!" cried Walter triumphantly. He undid his trousers with his free hand and extracted a rat. After wringing its neck and throwing it aside, he buttoned up his trousers and wiped the sweat from his brow. "Phew!" he said with relief, "it were a near go. I tremble to think of the damage that bugger might 'ave done."

Walter had omitted to tie string round the bottoms of his trousers. Now he tied string round them firmly, muttering, "It were a near go, by gum, it were a near go. What that old bugger might have done to me don't bear thinking on. I be all of a tremble. By gum, it were a near go."

All of us, I think, shuddered to think of what a rat might do up a trouser leg, and we bent down and checked the string around our trouser legs.

Uncle George was getting more behind with the sacks of corn. I counted seven, eight — no, I think it was nine, full sacks in a line, all of them untied. He appeared to be clumsy in his movements. I couldn't see him unhitching the full sacks from the thresher, but I could see him pulling the sacks on the truck from the machine and I saw his fat bottom bump the line of full sacks. Down went the whole line of them, one on top of the other, corn spilling out all over the barn floor amongst the chaff and straw. Fred came to his rescue and helped him pull the sacks upright, both of them scooping up as much corn as they could with their hands returning it to the sacks, but, of course, a lot still remained on the ground. Mr Saggamore noticed the wasted corn and made some caustic remarks.

"It were a little mishap," explained Uncle George.

"It was damned negligence," snapped Mr Saggamore.

"It were a pure accident," said Uncle George.

"Damned carelessness. Look at the amount you've wasted. Ruination, that's what it is. I can't allow this sort of tom-foolery to go on."

"Now, look here, Ernest, I ain't obliged to come and I ain't obliged to put up with that kind of talk," said Uncle George. "It's downright ingratitude after the way I've slogged my guts for you today. I've a mind not to come tomorrow, if that's the attitude you're gwain to take."

"Now, now," said Mr Saggamore in conciliatory tones.

"Don't you 'now, now' me, Ernest Saggamore," blustered Uncle George. "I byunt one of your reg'lar

173

chaps. It were a pure accident and you've no cause to speak to me in that rough manner."

"There's no need to get rasty, George."

"Rasty, be buggered! I've heaved my guts out today and all I get is abuse. I tell 'ee, I be right daggled."

"We don't want to fall out, George."

"Fall out be damned! You're a smart 'un to talk about fallin' out. I byunt fallin' out, I be tired out. 'Tis you who be doin' all the fallin' out," said Uncle George with an injured expression.

"Perhaps you'd like a change of job, George."

"I'd better 'ave a change of job if I be to remain here, 'cos I 'ouldn't do this un any more. No, I 'ouldn't, Ernest Saggamore, not if you went down on your bended knees I 'ouldn't."

"What about you taking over Jack's job, building the straw ricks?"

"Ah, now you'm talkin' some sense, Ernest. I bin lookin' at that rick and thinkin' old Jack ain't makin' much of a job of 'n. 'Im wants keepin' out well, but you con't tell them chaps like Jack anythin'. If you wants some bloody good ricks built you've got the right man here."

Thus placated, Uncle George agreed to build the straw ricks and the machinery was moved to the next bay.

"You want to keep the drum in tight to the bay of corn, Fred. You got a tendency to keep it a little wide," said Uncle George. "It makes extra work for Walt. You want to think of these little things you know."

Fred merely grunted and changed the corn riddle for barley.

174

"Make sure you've got the drum dead level, Fred," said Uncle George. Fred was having difficulty with the riddle. Eventually he had it fixed and turned round, his face very red and dusty.

"You want to back that tractor a bit more, Fred, or the driving belt won't be tight enough," said Uncle George.

"An' you wants to shut yer mouth, you bloody ol' puff guts," snarled Fred.

"Ah, you fill yer guts with my cider and then speak like that. You 'ouldn't do't if you was only sober," said Uncle George.

I walked over to where Mr Saggamore and Jack stood talking. Mr Saggamore put out a hand and gently rocked the cider cask. I heard him say to Jack, "Old George talks as though he've given us the cider and drinks most of it himself. And then to cap the lot he goes and wastes all that corn, but I don't want no bother with him. You look after the corn, Jack. I've persuaded him to see to the straw, he ought to be able to cope with that. It'll be a fresh rick he's starting, so if he falls he won't hurt himself much, 'cos that cider's already gone to his head and will be down in his legs soon."

We did about another hour's threshing before Fred called time. Then Mr Saggamore and Jack went to help with the milking and I fed the bullocks. When I had finished, I walked back past the Dutch barn. Everyone had now departed and the dust had settled. I could just see the threshing machine in the gloom; even now, still and silent, it resembled a monster. A rat scuttled in the bottom of the hedge as I walked across the fields, the moon and stars shone overhead and there was a sharp nip in the air. I felt tired and dirty and chilled.

Uncle George was waiting in his van near the farmhouse. "Put your bike in the back, my boy, and have a ride home," he said, puffing clouds of smoke from his pipe.

As I settled in the van and we drove away he said, "You can give me a hand to feed my pigs." The dust seemed still to be irritating Uncle George too; he sneezed and coughed most of the way home.

It was frosty again next morning and I felt utterly miserable with chilblain-swollen feet as I climbed to my position on the drum again. The barley was dirtier and dustier than the wheat, the awns irritated us and the air was thick with thistle down. Thistles stuck in my fingers. "You'll have a nice little job at nights, getting them out," said Frank, and smiled.

This morning seemed even longer than yesterday's. I refrained from asking Frank the time until I judged it was almost one o'clock. I wasn't sure which was worse, the coldness or the hunger. "What's the time?" I asked, confident it was almost one o'clock and time to stop. Frank pulled at the leather strap and drew forth his watch. "Twenty past eleven," he said. "You sure it hasn't stopped?" "They all say that," he said, returning the watch to his pocket.

Walter leaned over the side of the stack, gripping the stanchion with one hand. The other hand he cupped to the side of his mouth and bellowed, "Hey, George, the wind's blowing thy rick over."

Uncle George shook a fist at him and continued with his work. A little later I saw him carrying some props which he pushed under the leaning rick. Soon the rick began to lean the other way and more props were brought and pushed under that side. Jack strolled round to have a look and shouted, "You oughta have had a rick mould, George." Fred, on his round with cider jar, told everyone that George's rick had so many legs that it would be sure to walk away.

Bill, hearing all the comments, came to the side of the rick to look down and see what all the fuss was about. "Oho, thy rick's goin' to topple any time, ain't it, George?"

This remark from Bill, together with the prolonged cackle of a laugh, was too much for Uncle George. He had put up with the leg-pulling with a good grace, but now he could endure no more. His face went the colour of one of his beloved beetroots as angrily he thrust his pike into the rick and climbed down the ladder. Walter stopped work and leaned on his pike and watched him. I turned my head and saw Uncle George approach Mr Saggamore.

I be a-gwain home," stormed Uncle George. "I byunt gwain to put up with no more on't. I byunt obliged to come and I ain't workin' for money. All as I be gettin' is a snotty bit of tail corn."

Mr Saggamore put a hand on Uncle George's shoulder and said something quietly to him.

"Saggamore's givin' yer Uncle a bit of wet talk," said Frank.

"I byunt gwain to put up with their gyulin'," roared Uncle George. "I've never experienced the like on't before and I'm damned if I be gwain to have it now. If they all got on with their work instead of actin' like a lot of kids, it'd be a damn sight more sense."

Mr Saggamore said something else to him and whatever it was, it seemed to have a soothing effect.

"We never 'ad this kind of shindig at Clutterbuck's," said Uncle. "I allus work on the bay with Walter an' we get on like a house afire."

A few more quiet words from Mr Saggamore and a broad grin spread over Uncle's face. "Ah," he chuckled, "let Bill build the rick if he's so bloody clever, and I'll work on the mow with old Walt."

A muttering Bill was sent to the straw rick. Uncle George climbed on to the bay of barley, grasped a pike and roared, "Come on, you chaps, get to work. Put yer hacks into's, there's bin enough bloody time wasted."

When we stopped at one o'clock, I heard Mr Saggamore say to Jack, "Old George is a funny old bugger, but I don't want any bother with him. I don't know as I'll be any too keen to have him another time."

Today Uncle George did not join the others under the straw rick, but sat chewing morosely in his van. Feeling rather sorry for him, I went and sat in the van beside him.

"I don't want to sit with they chaps," he said, scattering crumbs over his chin and lap. "That Bill Lugg sat by me yesterday and where he'd got hot he stunk like a fitcher. His shirt was open at the neck and I could see the dirt on his chest an' it weren't fresh dirt neither. He don't wash from one month to another. I know all them Luggs, they be a dirty lot. Old Bill's like an 'airy ape."

Uncle George cut his cold bacon with a pocket knife and looked thoughtful. "What's that you got?" he said looking at my food. "Bread an' cheese! That ain't no good to work on, I'll bring you some of my bacon tomorrow. They gutsy beggars 'ave drunk most of the cider I brought."

A long pause. We continued eating, Uncle putting wadges of bread and bacon in his mouth with the aid of the blade of his knife. Suddenly he brightened, "I tell you what, I'll bring a jar of my perry tomorrow, just for you and me."

Uncle finished eating and took a good swig of cider from a bottle and then handed it to me.

"I'll hang back tonight, give you a hand with the cattle. Ernest have told me to take a couple of sacks of corn home tonight. So when they chaps be cleared off we'll load it into the van. It don't do to let them sort of fellas know too much." Uncle George screwed up his face, puckered his eyes, rubbed the side of his nose and looked very knowing.

"That Fred's a common, coarse, low sort of a fellow. And he's living with some low, vulgar sort of woman. But even she won't stick him for long, none on 'em do."

He filled his pipe and lit it and started to cough and splutter. "That dust ain't doin' me any good, I'll have to have some Friar's Balsam tonight — Frank's a decent enough fella, too good to be workin' along the likes of that there Fred, the foul-mouthed varmint. Look at 'un! Look at 'un!"

I looked in the direction Uncle George pointed and saw Fred standing by the cask, drinking.

"Abuse me left, right and centre, and then guzzle my cider. I hope it do choke 'un."

Uncle removed the pipe from his mouth and pouted his lips in disgust.

"I never knowed Jack Musgrove was that kind of fella, but he showed himself up in his true colours this morning. I shan't forget it in a hurry either. But it's old Walt I be most surprised in, allus thought him to be a tidy chap. Allus got on well with him at Clutterbuck's. I suppose it's 'cos he've got in with bad company here."

Fred started the tractor, we got out of the van. Uncle George beckoned me to his side and whispered confidentially, "I shouldn't have too much to do with some on 'em if I was you. They ain't the sort of people to get too familiar with. Scrim-scrankers I do call 'em."

We finished the barley at three o'clock and Fred started to move the tackle to a bay of oats.

Fred's boss, the owner of the threshing tackle, arrived with some drums of vaporising oil. "Where the bloody 'ell you bin to?" snarled Fred, his face flushed with exertion and cider. "'Ave you bin asleep these last dree or fower days? I should 'ave bin right out of oil by tonight, and what would I 'ave done then, eh?" The owner of the thresher did not speak, he just stood with his hands in his pockets.

"Where the 'ell you bin? What 'ave you bin coin'? What kind of a way is that to go on, eh, eh?" rasped Fred. His boss just smiled and took a dirty crumpled cigarette packet from his pocket. "Here, have a fag, Fred."

Without thanking him, Fred took a cigarette and stuck it in his mouth. "Oh no you don't," said Mr Saggamore. "I'm not having you smoking in here. You'll have the whole barn afire."

180

"No, I wun't," said Fred, producing an oily box of matches and waggling his head. "What about when you 'ad the steam engine a-dreshing and sending up sparks?"

"You ain't smoking in here," replied Mr Saggamore.

"Oh, all right," said Fred with an ill grace and poked the cigarette behind his ear.

"Well, I'll be off now," said the owner of the tackle.

"So long," grunted Fred, "and don't be so bloody long a-comin' next time."

Fred had difficulty getting the tackle lined up and in getting the drum level. He pulled the drum with the tractor at one end and Jack, Bill and I caught hold of the tow-bar at the other end to steer. We couldn't quite get the drum in the right position and because of a drop in the ground, Fred had to jack the drum up a bit on the one side. Fred came round to the three of us and cursed. When he was safely out of the way, Bill lifted the heavy iron tow-bar high above his head, and then, stepping back quickly, let it crash to the ground. "There," he said with evident satisfaction, "that's to show the bugger I ain't frightened of 'im."

When we finished for the day, Uncle George refused to say goodnight to the others when they called goodnight to him. He just grunted and went and sat in his van. And then, just when they were moving away, he wound the window down and shouted, "You wun't be seein' me termorrer."

The following morning, while I was cutting hay for the bullocks, I heard Mr Saggamore and Jack talking in the barn.

"I hope there's no rumpus today, Jack. I hope we can get on like other people."

"We ain't doin' too bad."

"Old George is a funny old customer, he've got to be handled just right. You'd never believe to hear him talk, that I bought that cider off him, gave him every penny he asked too. And promised him an extra bag of corn, just to keep him sweet. Then he goes and drinks most of it hisself, well, him and that Fred. That Fred gets the cider down him and gets that nasty and quarrelsome by about three o'clock. D'you hear the way he spoke to his boss yesterday?"

"George said just as we left last night, that he wasn't coming today.

"I hope he does, or we'll be short-handed. Caleb won't be able to put in much time. He's got to get a load of kale for the cows."

When I walked into the driveway of the barn they were putting some sacks of corn on top of others. "It's a good malting sample, Jack," said Mr Saggamore. "Ah, it's bright," replied Jack. Mr Saggamore slapped a sack of barley with the palm of his hand. "I think everything 'ould come to a standstill if there weren't any beer." He paused, slapped another sack and said emphatically, "It seems as if beer's more important than bread."

By now Fred and several others had arrived. As Fred filled the tractor with water he asked, "Where's Jarge?"

"'Im said 'im weren't coming today, aye 'im did," answered Bill. For some reason Bill looked goggle-eyed as he spoke — perhaps he thought he'd be blamed for Uncle George's absence.

"I'd aim as you must 'ave offended'n, Toby," said Fred. Toby looked confused, his face reddened and he struggled to say, "I never had a cross word with him."

"Here he is," shouted Walter a moment later. We all looked and saw the little blue van coming up the frozen field. Fred switched the petrol on and caught hold of the starting handle of the tractor. Walter pointed to the tractor and remarked, "Them yally 'uns never was no good." Fred glared at him and snarled, "Aarh, aarh."

Uncle George squeezed out of the van and walked towards us, smiling broadly, all bonhomie. "Good morning," he said in that rich, fruity voice. His face was creased in smiles, even his eyes sparkled. I had never seen him look more benevolent. "I've decided to let bygones be bygones," he rumbled, "and I've brought some of my cold, boiled bacon. There's plenty for everyone. I thought last night, 'Them chaps want summat better'n bread an' cheese to work on. No wonder they got a bit niggly and bad tempered.' And I've brought a few jars of perry to have with it."

The tractor roared to life, Fred put the pulley into gear, flap-flap-flap, flapflap, went the driving belt. Another day's threshing had begun.

We almost finished the first bay of oats by one o'clock. There were a lot of mice towards the bottom and they'd chewed the strings of the sheaves through, so that Walter had a lot of loose stuff to pitch up and a lot of it tumbled back down on him. There was a strong smell of mice. "Phew," Walter said, "them mice do stink like old 'ooman's pee."

Today Uncle George sat with everyone else by the straw rick. "Help yourselves to bacon, there's plenty there," he said. "And don't stint yourselves with the perry, I brought it to be drunk. And if I have to take any of that bacon home I shall be offended. Here, Toby, my boy, a little bit like that's no good to you, cut a gurt slice."

"It's damn good bacon, George," said Fred.

"It is that," said the others.

"Help yourselves," said Uncle George. "Cut another slice, Frank. Come on, Jack, have some more. Pour yourself some more perry, Fred, but go careful with it, you know what perry's like."

"The beer ain't like it used to be," said Jack.

"It ain't worth the money these days," said Walter.

"I remember when beer was tuppence 'alfpenny a pint," said old Mr Williams. "And it were beer then." With a far-away look in his eyes, he shook his head mournfully.

"There's nobody like the boss for growing barley," said Jack.

"Arthur Clutterbuck can grow barley," said Walter, in a tone that denied argument.

"Tuppence 'alfpenny a pint an' good, strong beer," said old Mr Williams wistfully. "Or five pints for a shillin'. They used to tell the tale about the fellow who'd spent all night at the pub and when he got home he thought he saw two candles burning. So he says to his missus, 'There I've been bustin' my guts to save a 'alfpenny and here you be, squanderin' money by burnin' two candles.'"

The men moved away from the straw and began pulling out packets of cigarettes. "No, no," cried Uncle George. "Here you are, have one of mine." He pushed a packet of twenty cigarettes towards them. Old Mr Williams, who didn't smoke, shook his head and muttered, "Real beer it were then," like one in a trance. Bill was the last to take a cigarette and Uncle George handed the packet to him, saying, "You keep 'em, Bill, I never smoke the things."

"Real beer in them days," muttered Mr Williams to no one in particular. "Nothin' but water and chemicals, that's all it is," he said in a louder voice.

"Salt," said Walter, "Salt. I knew a man who was gardener to a brewer and he was allus bringing him salt to put on the garden. 'Course he got it from the brewery. They put plenty of salt in the beer to make you thirsty and drink more of it.

"Dree white frosts, it'll rain tomorrow," stated Frank.

"If it's wet, I shan't come," said old Mr Williams, "the wet weather do play my rheumatics up somethin' crool."

Fred looked at his watch. "Time to start," he said, "and 'ere's the boss a-coming."

Frank was right. The weather broke and we had heavy rain all through the night. The fields were sodden next morning and we sloshed and squelched our way across them. Frank had to leave his motorbike by the roadside, and Uncle George his van. The ditches gushed with water, the trees and hedges dripped with rain. The sky looked pale and watery, black clouds drifted, the sun glimmered timidly. The whole world had a washed-out appearance.

On arrival, Fred looked up at the sky, his face contorted, and out of the side of his mouth he rasped, "I should think the bloody sky 'ave opened its arse-hole."

Fortunately everyone could work under cover; the oat straw was being stacked in the bays vacated by the wheat and barley. In the afternoon the tackle had to be moved to a stack of beans outside. By then it was dry overhead, but the wheels of the thresher sank deeply into the soft earth. Fred used the winch to pull it, but even so the rest of us had to heave and dig. We managed to move it, yard by yard, but even so tempers got frayed.

"If you'd put her on some sleepers, we'd never have had all this fuss," said Uncle George.

"We ain't got no sleepers," said Jack.

"I said 'if'. If you'd put her on sleepers. If, Jack, if," reasoned Uncle George.

"If," said Jack. "If. If yer auntie'd had balls, 'er'd a bin yer uncle."

"Oh, that's the way it is, is it?" said Uncle George. "Make a civil remark and get an answer like that."

Uncle stopped pushing and wagged a finger at Jack. "Jack Musgrove, I allus used to think you was a decent sort of a chap, but, rajah rhubarb, I'm beginnin' to change my mind."

"C'mon George, put thy beef into it and if we all do the same we'll shift it," said Walter.

"You're right there, Walt, I wish you'd tell Jack that. All this talkin's no bottle," replied Uncle George.

Once the tackle was in place beside the bean stack, Jack and Bill climbed on to the rick and began to strip off the thatch. "Don't chuck them pegs all over the place," Mr Saggamore shouted to Bill, who was throwing them down willy-nilly.

"That's the trouble with some of these chaps today," said Uncle George severely. "Got no sense."

The hard brittle bean haulm made my fingers sore. The haulm was so long that Frank had difficulty in feeding it into the drum. Inside the drum the beans rattled and occasionally one shot out of the drum and hit my face. The threshed haulm was not tied, but stacked loose. Later, like the wheat and barley straw, it would be used for bedding; the oat straw for feeding.

The full sacks of beans were placed on some straw to keep them dry. I saw Mr Saggamore slap one and say, "No beast'll ever pay to yut that at the price it's fetching." When we had finished threshing for the day the remaining bean stack was covered with a large tarpaulin, tied, and weighted down with logs. The threshed beans were loaded into a dung cart. Two men to a sack, each grabbing a bottom corner, the other hands clasped behind the sack, and then heaved into the cart. "What you need is a short piece of strong stick," said Walter, going off in search of a piece while Jack and I were lifting the sacks into the cart. "When the bottoms reach the cart, give 'em a good pound," Jack told me. The sacks were heavy; two and a quarter hundredweights, the same as wheat, barley weighing two hundredweights and oats only one and three-quarter hundredweights to the four bushels. I had great hopes of Walter's stick method.

Walter returned with a short length of a pike handle, a handle that had been broken. He'd sawn the end off

187

neatly. Instead of clasping hands, we now caught hold of the stick behind the sacks, but we still had to lift, heave and "give 'em a pound".

I expressed my disappointment in the stick and Jack said, "Ah, there's no easy way, you still need muscle, brute force and ignorance." He wasn't quite right about ignorance; lifting sacks, like most farm jobs, required skill. The maximum effort with the minimum amount of energy. It looked deceptively easy and simple, the way the farmworkers did it. And it was this skill, this apparently slow and effortless labour, I suppose, that had led so many country writers and poets to speak of "only men lifting sacks", or "only a man ploughing". Had they done the work themselves, instead of just observing and writing of it, they would have found it required skill and effort and wasn't so slow either. Then perhaps they would have omitted the word "only".

"Now, a good pound, and we'll have this one right on top," said Jack, when he'd fastened the tail board.

"That's right," said Uncle George, sitting on one of the unloaded sacks and puffing contentedly at his pipe, "you heave and I'll grunt."

Saturday morning we moved to a stack of wheat. It was less dusty working in the open, and warmer too, we hadn't the cutting draught we had in the barn. Toby's work was easier as he hadn't so far to move the chaff. With the milder weather my chilblains had disappeared and though the work was still hard and dusty, perhaps because I was getting used to it, I almost came to enjoy it. But really it was the company which made it bearable; I think everyone felt this.

On Monday, Mr Saggamore said to Frank, "This is some good wheat straw — I want to put a little rick of it by for thatching, so put it through the drum especially careful."

Towards the bottom of the wheat stack were many rats. We'd been able to put the wire up more effectively round the outside stacks. Uncle George and Walter were able to kill dozens with their pikes. Fred got on the stack and joined in the slaughter, but even so, the wire only being about two feet high, many of the rats jumped off the stack and right over the wire.

At mid-day on Tuesday we finished. Fred counted the sacks of wheat (as required by the War Ag), and said to Mr Saggamore, "I ain't counted 'em too near." I saw Mr Saggamore take a pound note out of his breeches pocket and hand it to him. Later I saw Frank and Walter pocketing notes.

"I'll get it over to the house for you, George," said Mr Saggamore.

"Thank you," said Uncle George. He rubbed the side of his nose and rumbled, "My stock'll be all right for a while now."

I looked round at the straw ricks, the wheat chaff which would be used to mix with the sliced roots. The pile of useless barley awns, the discarded thatch, the corpses of rats, the ruts, the mud, the muddles and rubbish. The thistles in my hands were festering. I watched Fred slowly winching his tackle down the field, and, in a way, I was almost sorry to see them go.

CHAPTER
NINE

The arts of husbandry

Mr Saggamore took samples of wheat and barley to market. He put handfuls of the corn in little bags which were small enough to stuff in the voluminous pockets of his chequered market jacket. The bags were black, the better to show the brightness of his corn.

Jack, Bill and I hauled straw into the cattle sheds and yards, load after load, until the straw lay two or three feet deep. The following day we brought cattle into the yards from the fields which were now so wet and trodden.

Undoubtedly, a field of clean, level, ripening corn, particularly wheat, was the sight that most gladdened a farmer's eye. But a yard of fat cattle, contentedly chewing their cuds, and with straw up to their bellies, would rank a close second. During weekdays we had no time to stand and stare, but on succeeding Sunday mornings during the winter, after we'd fed and littered the cattle, Mr Saggamore and I stood and stared. We stood and leant upon the rails, one foot on the lower rail, and looked at the cattle. The air on a still morning was redolent with the aroma of sliced roots, the sweet fragrance of hay and the breath of the beasts. When we put fresh straw beneath their feet, the cattle jumped and

190

frolicked. "That shows they're doing," observed Mr Saggamore. Then they returned to their troughs or cribs; long rough tongues scooping up the last of the roots, crushed oats and bean meal; steady munch, munch, as they pulled the hay from the racks and ate it. Replete, they would turn and stand chewing their cuds and then flop down and lie in the clean dry straw, grunting. One still standing might lift its tail: plop, plop, plop, went its muck. "That's how I like to see their dung," Mr Saggamore would say, "like porridge, they're healthy when their dung's like that."

I learnt much from Mr Saggamore on these Sunday mornings when, to all intents and purposes, we only stood and stared. "There's an art in feeding cattle," he told me. "They must have plenty of good grub, but they must never be allowed to lose their appetite. The fatter they get, the more choosy they get. Old Bill's got no idea, he'll have more hay under their feet than in their rack. Too much bean meal and they'll scour and go off their food. Roots must be well cleaned before they're pulped, cattle won't eat dirt. If I didn't keep on at him, old Bill 'ould never clean their mangers out, he'd flop food down on dung and expect 'em to eat it."

Mr Saggamore showed me the points of a beef animal. "There, that's what I call a good beast, look at his hind-quarters. See the difference between him and that'n there." He pointed to a mottle-faced bullock. "He's what I call a goosey-arsed 'un — got no backside, he'll never make a first-class beast. And that un over there in the corner ain't doin' 'cos the others bully him and drive him away from his grub." (Cattle at this time still carried their horns, and the weak and timid were literally driven to the wall.)

"If we moved him . . ." I suggested.

"There'd be another driven away tomorrow," replied Mr Saggamore "It's a funny thing, but they'll always pick on one and drive him away.

Drinking troughs were positioned to catch rain water from the roofs of the buildings, but in dry weather we had to carry all the water to these cattle in buckets from the pool. And a couple of score of cattle can drink an awful lot of water. In frosty weather they seemed to drink even more.

"Before the war, Mr Troy said he could've laid water on from the other buildings for a hundred pounds," mused Mr Saggamore one day. "I wish I'd had it done now."

We spent hours during the winter carrying water. Jack was always hoping it might rain, often saying in the afternoon, "I don't think I'll carry any more, it might rain during the night." But it was a mistake not to carry sufficient, as the cattle only drank even more next day, sucking the troughs dry before you could even move from the troughs after tipping the water in. On the whole, however, labour meant little or nothing to most farmers. They seemed to go out of their way to make more work instead of lessening it. Long hours and hard work were the supreme virtues. If you worked long and hard everything was bound to be all right, it was as simple as that in their minds. It was of little consequence, because they never gave it a thought, whether the long hours and hard labour were productive or profitable, or even useful. It would have been heresy to have questioned it, or to have suggested the time could have been put to better use. They believed implicitly in the slogan often found on old cider cups, "Industry produces wealth", though their experiences between the wars should have given them reason to doubt it.

To them farming was a way of life; they farmed by instinct, bred of generations, scorning the text-book wisdom of the experts. Their guidelines were of sight, touch and scent and an age-old wisdom. Their measurements were of the handful or the double-handful, the pitchful or the forkful, the cart or the wagon load. You judged their prosperity, not by their personal appearance, but by their fields and the condition of their livestock. They knew exactly the right time and way to perform every farming operation — I'm speaking now of the better farmers. To them farming was not only a way of life, but the whole of their life. "There are no crafts in the country and there is no culture," complained the author of *Four Years' Harvest*. Certainly there was little or no appreciation of books, music, painting. But it would be a mistake to overlook the several skills and arts of husbandry; had not William Cobbett declared agriculture the basis of all culture?

Cutting kale was a slow and unpleasant task. On frosty mornings we got cold and wet and on wet mornings we got cold and drenched. The kale leaves held the slivers of ice or water until we bent down and hacked at the kale stalks, thick as a man's arm, and as the great plants shook, their leaves showered us with ice or water,

193

usually both. The ruts along the headland became deeper, the mud was worse than at sugar beet time.

We took the loads of kale to the cowshed. It was a two-man job cutting the kale with the pulper, one pushing the kale down into the pulper, the other turning the handle.

"Rugman feeds his kale whole to the cows. Chucks it out in the fields to 'em," said Jack.

"I don't grow good grub to have it tramped in the mud," said Mr Saggamore.

Jack put hedging gloves, an axe, a bill hook and a stake beetle into an old food sack and slung it over his shoulder. I caught hold of another axe and two hedge bills and put them on my shoulder. I put out my other hand and picked up a bow saw. "You don't want saws, hedging," said Jack severely.

A pile of willow stakes, sharpened at the bottom, and chamfered at the tops to prevent splitting, were lying by the hedge to be laid. Starting at the top of the field, we first "ridded out" a length of the hedge, that is, we cut out the briars and brambles and all the wood not wanted for laying. Then Jack started laying, preaching the hedge near its base by making a long, sloping cut so that it would lie down easily. "Preach down to the ground, that's the way. If you don't, next time the hedge is laid you've got a lot of stumps and the fresh wood growing from 'em. You can't make a tidy job of a hedge like that. And if it ain't pleached low the sheep can get under the hedge."

Jack laid the preachers uphill and cut off the snags left from the pleaching. He drove stakes in at a slight angle, their tops inclining slightly towards the unlaid hedge. "Always use a stake bittle, you won't split the stakes then. I've seen some fellows use their axes and the tops of their stakes look like shaving brushes.

The stake beetle was one piece of wood, its head large and clublike, hollowed out to take the head of the stake. Jack was always on the lookout for a likely piece of wood with the requisite clump to fashion into a stake "bittle".

"Never bend a live stick," said Jack, laying a piece of hawthorn down among the stakes. The brush (the tops) was all laid down the same side of the hedge. "Some do use an iron bar to make holes for their stakes," said Jack, driving more stakes in, "but I can mostly get 'em in without splittin'. Of course, if we was goin' to ether the hedge, we'd put the stakes in upright."

Ethering was weaving long thin sticks, usually hazel, along the tops of the stakes. "You put a stick to every stake," said Jack, "some don't and then wonder why their ethering's a mess."

Mr Saggamore came to see how we were getting on. "You're making a good job of that, Jack," he said. "That'll be something for 'em to look at as they come along the road. Father was a good hedger, he still does a bit, even at his age."

Most of the wood in the hedge was hawthorn, which we called "quick", though there was some hazel also. "Quick's the stuff for a hedge, that'll make a fence. No barbed wire nor nothin' needed with a quick hedge. That ellum's no good, it's no fence and it don't matter how thin you preach it, it'll spring back up," said Jack.

We were not far from the Misses Putterill's smallholding. Miss Hannah was out sawing firewood on a saw-horse. "Her's havin' two warms out of that wood," said Jack, "one while 'er's sawing it an' another when 'er burns it." We watched her for a moment and when she had almost sawn a piece through, she hit it with the teeth of the saw to break it. "See that?" asked Jack. "You'll have to bring her another saw in a day or two at that rate. It's awful, ain't it? Sometimes the two on 'em gets on a cross-cut and they'd push when they ought to be pullin'."

In the field next door to us, right in front of the Putterills', were the milking cows and the Hereford bull. Mr Saggamore was always telling us, "If you see the old bull trying to serve a cow, drive 'em away 'cos of them two women." I saw the bull serving a cow and mindful of Mr Saggamore's instructions, suggested we should move them. "Lar, bless you," said Jack, "I d'aim they do like to see it."

Mr Cordwell came along the road on a bicycle. Seeing us, he dismounted and inspected our work. "Tidy job, Jack, tidy job," he said. "But down in Berkeley we never used stakes 'cos of the huntin'. You can lay a hedge without stakes, you know."

"Ah," said Jack, a bit nettled, "and I can lay a hedge with stakes, as good as any man."

"If you didn't use stakes, you'd save your boss a tidy bit of money. It costs money to cut stakes, you know. Now, if you laid it without stakes, it would be cheaper."

"Ah," said Jack, when Mr Cordwell had gone, "if his auntie had had balls, she'd have bin his uncle. Comin'

196

and tellin' me how to lay a hedge. Never does any hedge layin' up at his place, he've got hedges as high as houses and the stock walk right through 'em."

The cold east winds of March dried the mud of winter and the earth began to crumble. Dust rose behind the heavy harrows cultivating the ground for oats and barley.

"A peck of dust in March," observed Jack, "is worth a king's ransom."

The ground on which the kale had stood was ploughed and cultivated; the kale stumps had to be collected and taken away by the cart-load. "I won't grow any more kale," grumbled Mr Saggamore.

The ring of the Cambridge rolls was a familiar sound everywhere. When the corndrill was lifted at the headlands the coulters came up dry and shining. "Wheat in mud, barley in dust," said Jack, ever ready with an adage.

But the coldness persisted; hedges were still bare, what little grass there was looked blue and shrivelled. When the drilling was finished Mr Saggamore said, "We need a little warm rain."

The winter wheat was harrowed, breaking up the hard crust of winter. Across the drills went the harrows, tearing the wheat and covering much of it with the broken earth. The result looked disastrous, but Mr Saggamore looked at it with approving eyes. "Wheat likes to be treated rough," he said. "Never be afraid of ripping it about, that'll encourage it to tiller well. But it 'ouldn't do for oats or barley."

Suddenly the spring arrived, the all-pervading spring. The hedges were tinged with green and in the elm trees, now clothed with shy leaves like mouse ears, the young rooks were clamorous in the nest their parents had repaired while the elm trees had swayed in those biting winds of March.

Chain harrows chattered up and down the pastures, leaving alternate strips of light and dark green. Cattle still yarded grew restless, smelling the scent of spring, eager for the food and freedom of the pastures. Warm showers brought the fragrance of the earth, the sun was like a caress.

The oats and barley stood boldly in drill and the winter wheat caught in a gust of wind looked like dark green waves sweeping over the field.

The lambs grew; now they had to bend their front legs to suckle their mothers, nuzzling and bunting, their tails waving ecstatically. They forsook their mothers to frisk and frolic together in the orchard, now canopied with the white lace of plum blossom and carpeted with dark green grass and wild daffodils. They played follow my leader, skipped, jumped on or over a fallen tree trunk and wore the grass away in a hollow, and at dusk the air filled with the plaintive cries of the ewes calling their young.

Theo Biddle came to "tail" them and castrate the ram lambs. Red-faced Theo, who had a smallholding, was the local castrator, his father having had him apprenticed to the trade. There was a certain fussiness about Theo. "Have you got plenty of dry wood for the fire?" he asked as he slowly dismounted from his bicycle. "Have you got the fire going well?" he said as he untied his small leather bag containing his tools from the carrier on the back of his bicycle. "It ain't any good unless you've got plenty of heat in the heart of it."

The ewes and lambs penned in a corner of the orchard were making a hubbub. Ewes which had temporarily lost sight of their young and lambs looking for parents were searching and calling. "Have you got them securely penned?" said Theo, alarmed eyes darting apprehensively. "If they break out we'll have a hell of a caper. I can't afford to stop here all day chasing sheep."

He put two of his irons in the fire. "I wouldn't do it if the moon weren't right. No. No matter what you paid, I wouldn't do it if the moon weren't right. You got a bucket and water handy? That bench is a bit low, but no matter, no matter, I'll manage somehow. How are those irons?"

Theo took an iron out of the fire, glowing red, and held it a few inches from his cheek. Then he spat on it and said, "That's all right, can't work with cold irons. Right, Bill, catch the first one, I can't afford to hang about here all day."

Bill caught the first lamb and handed it to me. "What is it? Ah, a ewe lamb," said Theo and directed me to the bench. Sitting on the bench I held the lamb, front left and hind left legs in one hand and its right legs similarly in my other, with its back against my chest. "Bring her forward a bit, so that her tail lies flat on the bench," instructed Theo. The hot iron was thrust down on to and through the tail. Sizzle, pop and crunch as the iron severed the tail, a smell of burning flesh, gristle and wool. Thin jets of blood spurted from the end of the stump of tail left on the lamb. Theo cauterised it with his iron and I released the lamb.

"That's a ram," said Theo when I took the next lamb from Bill. Holding it by the legs in the same fashion as before I stood up and placed the struggling lamb on my shoulder. Theo nicked the purse with his knife and bending towards it drew the testicles out with his teeth.

"Don't let those lambs lie down on the wet earth for the rest of the day," said Theo, when the last of the lambs was done. "They'll be that stiff in the morning they won't be able to walk. Keep walking them about. They'll catch cold on that wet earth, come out every hour or so and stir them up."

Bill put the severed tails in a sack. "Our Mother'll cook they for us, aye her will. I like lambs' tail and so does our Gritt."

"Douse that fire," ordered Theo, "and we'll go and see to those bull calves."

Jack had a fire burning against a wall; Theo gave it an approving look as we went into a shed containing a dozen bull calves. The calves ranged from four to six months and were well grown for their age — all the calves at Suttridge were reared on nurse cows — Mr Saggamore believed a quart of milk from the cow was worth a gallon from the bucket.

"Too big," said Theo, placing a bucket and his tools on top of the wall. "Why does he let 'em get so big before he sends for me? There's no sense in it, no sense at all. Heavin' our guts out catching and tushing 'em about. An' it knocks 'em back when they're so big," grumbled Theo, tying his rope around the legs of a calf which Jack was holding by the nose in a corner of the shed.

"When I pull and he falls," said Theo to me, "catch hold of the rope tight and put your foot on his neck."

I held the animal as instructed and Theo grasped its testicles. He cut the purse, withdrew the testicles and placed his clamp behind them. "If he'd called me a week later I wouldn't have come. The flies, y'know." Bill handed him the saucer containing the lard and dark green ointment "There's no sense in it," muttered Theo. "I shan't do any more for him again if he lets 'em get so big. Look at the horns on this un, lucky he didn't knock the one off when he fell."

Theo smeared lard over the clamp and the cords of the testicles. Bill handed him one of the hot irons and Theo held it a couple of inches from his cheek before pressing it firmly down on the cords of the testicles held in the clamp. I heard the sizzle of lard and smelt burning flesh. Theo rubbed the green ointment into the wound and then pulled the rope free from the calf's legs and slapped him on the rump. "There," he said, as it rose slowly to its feet, "that's taken the boldness out of you, m'lad."

Bill and I penned the others in a corner and Jack made a swift pounce, catching another and holding it firmly with fingers and thumb in its nose.

"It's risky cuttin' 'em when they're as big as this," said Theo. "If I've told him once, I've told him a dozen times, but he don't hearken. If he loses one perhaps he'll listen. I wouldn't do 'em at all if the moon wasn't right."

201

"We've got some smaller ones in the next shed for you, aye us 'ave," said Bill.

"I hope they are," said Theo, dropping the handle of the iron and the severed testicles in the bucket half full of water, the water now tinged with blood. "I don't relish being pulled to flickuts by another dose like this. Put some more wood on the fire, Bill."

We caught the rest of the calves and Theo castrated them, his face wet with sweat. "It makes the fat run out of you, handling strong animals like this," he said.

When we had finished, Theo told Bill to put out the fire. Bill tipped a drop of water out of the bucket containing the testicles over the fire. "That ain't no good," said Theo severely, "I could piddle more'n that. Go and get a good bucketful and douse it, I've seen some damage done by leaving a fire smouldering."

Theo packed his tools in the little round black leather case and strapped it to his carrier on the back of his bicycle. "Put plenty of clean dry straw under 'em and don't let 'em lie down for long," he instructed, "or they'll get as stiff as the devil's nose and they won't be able to walk in the morning."

He wheeled his bicycle out to the road and mounted it, saying, "I'm goin' to have a pint of beer after all that struggling."

"Tie the horse up there," said Mr Saggamore. It was evening and we'd been horse-hoeing the roots for the first time. He led me across a couple of fields, a slight breeze blowing in our faces. "Hush," he said, putting a finger to his lips, as we approached a hedge, "and tread softly." We crept up to the hedge, our backs bent. "Now, quickly," he whispered, and we carefully peered over the hedge and saw fox cubs playing in the green wheat. We gazed in silence for perhaps fifteen or twenty minutes.

At that end of the wheat field there was a long, high bank. A bank of thick, rich red clay and on top of it a hedge with trees: ash, wild cherry, young oaks, and sloe bushes. In this bank lived foxes, badgers, stoats, weasels and rabbits. And all of them, apparently, lived in perfect harmony. The foxes ate rabbits, but somehow I don't think they attacked rabbits who lived in the bank. The badgers were never, or rarely, seen, being nocturnal animals, but we saw the entrance to their home. Periodically they cleaned their homes out, depositing the old bedding of dried grass and straw outside the burrows. Later in the year they would do a certain amount of damage by rolling in the ripening corn. However, they were useful in digging out wasps' nests and eating the grubs. Whether they were impervious to wasp stings or just tough old customers who endured the stings for the love of the grubs, I don't know. By and large the badger minded his own business, but he was a much maligned animal, being accused, almost invariably wrongly, of raiding hen houses.

The vixen came out and, perhaps aware of our presence, ushered her cubs back into the bank. "Ain't they lovely," said Mr Saggamore as we walked back to the horse.

Soon we were singling roots again, backs bent and eyes on the tiny plants. Mr Saggamore, a cowslip in his buttonhole, said, "I love hoeing."

Sheep shearing, haymaking and harvest. This year we hadn't Mike and Johnny. Instead we had two German prisoners of war: Stephan, young and elegant, in a well-fitting short white jacket; and an older, burly man, who we called Big Willy. Big Willy had a small farm back in Germany and a wife and young children.

Big Willy could speak moderately good English, though Mr Saggamore thought it necessary to wave his arms about a lot when talking to him. This waving of arms became habitual with Mr Saggamore, he began to do it even when talking to us. Old Mr Williams, rather shaky now, came to see how the harvest was progressing. He, too, had his share of arm waving from Mr Saggamore. "I don't," complained Mr Williams later, "want none of that German talk." Meaning of course, the arm waving.

Big Willy watched Jack and Bill cutting round the corn with a hook and crook. "I can do that quicker," he said. "Give me a scythe." Mr Saggamore sent me to get a scythe. Big Willy fixed a hazel rod to it to catch the falling corn. He removed his shirt, exposing a broad bronzed back and chest. With rippling muscles and glistening back he quickly cut round the field, leaving neat sheaves for me to bind.

While we were stooking, Stephan went into the wood, and did not return. Mr Saggamore grew agitated. Big Willy grinned and said, "Gone, gone. No like the work. Not used to it like me."

Mr Saggamore became worried. "It's a serious matter, losing a prisoner. I'd better go and phone the camp."

"They told me to catch him," he said, when he came back from telephoning, "and lock him up in the barn. Now if that ain't a my eye of a tale, I don't know what is. How can we catch him if we don't know where he is?"

Big Willy smiled and said, "Don't worry. He'll be back when the lorry come to take us back to camp."

Stephan came out of the wood as Big Willy predicted, but he came no more to Suttridge. Big Willy stopped with us until Christmas, helping with the roots and threshing. At other times he dug ditches and fed animals, becoming a friend of us all, telling us about his farming and showing us snapshots of his wife and two little girls.

No one, not even Mr Saggamore, worked harder than Big Willy, but all the while he worked he had a faraway, wistful look. Thinking, no doubt, and longing for his wife, the little girls and that farm back in Germany.

CHAPTER
TEN

A chance meeting

Miss Crotcher lived in a large crumbling old house a few miles from Suttridge Farm. Like her house, Miss Crotcher had known better days, but owing to an improvident father and a feckless, spendthrift brother the family fortune was all gone. Death duties too were blamed, but, as Mr Saggamore observed, such families had never worked, knew no trade and never learnt to live within their means.

Father, Mother, brothers and sisters dead, Miss Crotcher was the last of the line. A large, manly woman, fifty-five or perhaps sixty years of age — one could picture her when young, at horse shows, shooting parties, or fox hunting, fearless at fences and always in at the kill — she still possessed that indomitable spirit, characteristic of many of the landed gentry; at Hunt Balls she would have been a buxom young woman who perspired freely when dancing. Or at point to point race meetings, striding along purposefully, with her gruff matter-of-fact voice and booming laugh.

Now, for her, there were no more social occasions. She had aged, but she still strode, her laugh was still loud and hearty and she shouted at everyone with that gruff voice. Not unkindly, you must understand, it was just her manner; short, sharp, staccato sentences, usually in the form of a question, but delivered as a pronouncement. She smoked incessantly — her fingers were stained almost black by nicotine. Local gossip had it that she also drank heavily. A vigorous, commanding woman, but not without humour or benignity; she had, when her circumstances were considered, "gone to pot" in rather an endearing way.

With no family and precious little money left, she had abandoned all pride in position, and taken to dog and goat breeding, lavishing all her love and pride on them and their pedigrees. She kept scores of cats too, but they had no pedigree — she appeared to take in every stray or unwanted cat in the neighbourhood.

If it hadn't been for the goats, I doubt if I should ever have known her, but because of them I made frequent trips to her place with horse and cart and loads of swedes, mangolds or hay. Mr Saggamore said she was a great nuisance, always on the telephone or visiting him with demands for her goats; but secretly, I think, he was flattered by her friendship, calling her "the lady from Compton Manor", and trying to speak in a genteel manner when in conversation with her.

Only Miss Crotcher and her companion — a shy little woman who spoke in a whisper and seemed to glide or flit silently about — lived in the old house. Neither of them took much trouble about housekeeping, that was obvious from the complete chaos of the place. Several times I had been taken into the room in which they lived and each time the room had been littered with books, newspapers, pedigree forms, dirty cutlery, crockery and so forth. Dirty boots and wellingtons in the hearth, buckets to catch rain from the leaking roof, the furniture covered with dust and cigarette ash, pictures askew and wallpaper torn and mouldering, and cobwebs clinging to the ceiling. Chairs and sofas well sprinkled with hairs from the cats and dogs that constantly lounged in them.

No account of war-time farming would be complete without at least a mention of wireworms. Once our old pastures were ploughed and they were deprived of their normal diet of grass roots, they devoured the roots of the newly planted corn. Where the infestation was heavy all the corn would be destroyed and the field would have to be replanted, when the voracious wireworms would attack again. Rolling was the prescribed, but ineffective, remedy.

Rabbits were also a great pest and though the War Ag employed men to trap them the number of rabbits was still large. They devoured the young corn, especially near woodlands, and acres of ground were unproductive. They ate roots and grass and fouled the land. Considering the amount of damage they did, and the shortage of meat, it is surprising that even greater efforts weren't made to trap them.

Some of the old pastures were comparatively free from wireworm and the rabbits did not over-run every field. Our ploughed pasture fields were very fertile and were capable of growing heavy crops, but a heavy crop of corn was often laid low by storms just before harvest. The binder would have to be driven one way only to "catch" the laid crop, or perhaps the farmer and his men would have to resort to scythes and sickles. But before a laid crop was ripe enough to harvest the wood pigeons would descend in their thousands and plunder the precious grain.

And once the corn was stacked it wouldn't be long before the rats moved in, usually when the weather turned wet and cold. Some years a farm would be reasonably free from rats, another year there'd be a plague of them.

This winter we had an infestation of rats, not merely the rats that skulked in the barns and were rarely seen or those that lived in the corn stacks and were only seen at threshing time, but an invasion of rats. Even during daylight we saw rats scuttling about in and around the buildings and stackyard.

Over and above the disease they carry and the damage they do, there is something peculiarly loathsome, something repulsive about rats. I never see one but I get a tingle of horror down my spine. They have a malevolent appearance, those glittering eyes, that long tail, and though they inhabit the filthiest places they somehow manage to keep themselves clean. The furtive way they slink about makes them all the more sinister, the more dreaded. We see them move quickly and silently, but we do not see their legs or feet; perhaps it is this as much as anything which has caused the innate horror.

Traps and poison did little to diminish them. The cats caught an occasional rat, but it takes a good cat to tackle a rat and even then they have to jockey themselves into the right position before they can successfully pounce. Reuben and his terriers accounted for a few score, but they appeared to multiply faster than Reuben could kill them.

When the mole catcher came he offered advice. "Go to the barber's and get a sackful of hair. Two sackfuls of hair. And if he ain't got enough go to another barber and get more hair. And stuff the hair down the rat holes, and the rats'll think there's a lot of humans about and clear off."

Mr Saggamore was sceptical about the mole catcher's plan and Jack remarked, "From what I can see of these rats they'd only drag the hair down into their holes an' make nests out of it an' breed faster than ever."

A dirty little man with a wispy moustache and a tattered raincoat several sizes too large for him called and tried to buy some empty sacks. On seeing several large rats he exclaimed, "Coo, Guv'nor, ain't you got some rats 'ere, ain't you got some rats 'ere! Why don't you get rid on 'em?"

Mr Saggamore explained the difficulties and the little man said, "You leave it to me, Guv'nor, you leave it to me. I'll cope with the varmints. You just give me a fiver, cheap at the price, considering the quantity of rats you got. You give me a fiver an' you won't see a rat here termorrer." And with that he lifted up the lid of a corn bin and with a shout, he thrust his head and shoulders into the bin, his feet left the ground and waggled in the air. He remained thus suspended for a few minutes. The bin contained ground corn and clouds of dust arose while the man waged some desperate struggle within. A shriek of excitement and the man returned to his feet, his hair and face covered with dust and cobwebs. In his hands he held a mouse which he gleefully proceeded to squeeze to death.

"There, there," he shouted, full of excitement and laughter. "What d'you think of that, Guv'nor? What d'you think of that?"

He held the squashed mouse aloft by its tail and started to hop about crying, "There, Guv'nor, look, I've caught a mouse already. You can see I mean business, you can see I'm as good as my word. Give me a fiver now and I'll set to this very instant."

Mr Saggamore was unimpressed and declined the little man's offer, remarking, after the man had left — and he was only persuaded to leave with some difficulty — 'Did you ever see anything so kiddish. Catching one little mouse and making all that fuss — and squashing it in his bare hands. If I'd been daft enough to give that little tow-rag a fiver, it would have been the last I'd have seen of him or my money and we'd still have had the rats."

Harry Wellington told me that his Uncle John never had rats at his mill. Uncle John wouldn't have rats at his mill and he didn't know what Uncle John would have said had he seen such a swarm of rats. Unfortunately he was unable to tell us what Uncle John would have done.

A few weeks after Christmas a dark, taciturn man came and said he'd heard about the rats and promised he would get rid of them for a fee of ten pounds.

"Ah," said Mr Saggamore, "I've heard that tale before, except that the price was five pounds."

"You set me the job and I'll guarantee you won't see a live rat here after ten days. I'll come back in a fortnight and if there's no rats you pay me ten pounds. If there's still rats here you don't pay me a penny piece. I can't say fairer than that, can I?"

"That's a fair bargain," said Mr Saggamore, "but how are you going to do it?"

"I've promised to get rid of the rats, that's a bargain," said the stranger. "How I do it is my trade secret and is no part of the bargain."

"Fair enough," said Mr Saggamore. "It's a deal."

Within ten days there wasn't a rat to be seen at Suttridge Farm. The Stranger came and collected his ten pounds and departed without giving his name and address.

A week or so later we saw Tom Prewett.

"Have you got any rats at your place?" he asked.

"No," said Mr Saggamore.

"Neither had I until a couple wiks ago," said Tom, "but now the place is swarming with 'em, bloody 'undreds of 'em. I can't make it out anyhow."

"They do say rats be like that, they come and go. Come from nowhere, all of a sudden like," said Mr Saggamore blandly, giving Jack and me a wink. "I wouldn't worry over much if I were you, Tom, like as not they'll disappear as sudden as they came."

Mr Saggamore was laid up with lumbago, and Mrs Saggamore summoned me to his bedroom. "Take your boots off and follow me upstairs," she said.

He looked strange lying in bed, one didn't associate Mr Saggamore with illness or lying in bed in daylight.

Or, for that matter, ever staying indoors during daylight, except for meals and Sunday afternoons between dinner and milking time.

"I've sold Captain," he told me. Captain was the horse that kicked. "The man will be here with a lorry for him about eleven. Don't say too much to him, he's a proper old horse coper and as fly as they come. Don't let on as the hoss do kick or he'll try and beat the price down. You get him out of the stable, put one of our halters on him and lead him up quickly into the lorry and tie him up in front."

Just after eleven a brown cattle lorry drew up and a little bent-up man got out of the passenger seat and knocked on the door of the house. Mrs Saggamore answered the door, spoke to the man and pointed towards me.

"Take the lorry down there, Billy boy," he said in a wheezy voice.

While Billy boy was backing the lorry, the man hobbled up to me. He was wearing the tightest pair of trousers I'd ever seen. They were so tight, you could see the outline of his legs. I wondered how he managed to get them on and off. On his head he wore a battered old bowler hat, green with mildew. "I hear the guv'nor's got a touch of the screws," he wheezed. "Is the hoss in the stable here?"

I nodded my head and opened the top of the stable door. "Get the tailboard down, Billy boy." The wheeze had almost become a croak, the old man coughed and spat out a great lump of phlegm.

I opened the bottom door, went inside and put the halter on Captain. I led the horse out, trying not to look frightened. "'E don't kick, do 'e?" asked the old man. "No," I answered and hoped my voice was steady. For a moment I thought the old man was going to lay a hand on the horse's hind-quarters — he'd kick then all right. So I led Captain quickly towards the lorry. The old man stepped back and squinted at the horse. "Ee, ee, ee, what do you think on 'im, Billy boy?" he said. "'Ave 'e got a bit of grease d'you think?" I led the horse up the tailboard lest the old man should be tempted to run his hand down the horse's fetlock. The horse went up the tailboard quietly enough and I tied his head up at the front. Now I was faced with the tricky bit, how was I going to get past the horse's hindlegs without being kicked? I felt like shouting, "Any minute now I'm about to be kicked through the side of Billy boy's lorry." Instead I held my breath and sidled past the horse.

"Close the gates and pick up the tailboard, Billy boy," wheezed the old man. I helped Billy boy lift the tailboard up; I felt sorry for him, guessing he'd be next to walk past Captain's treacherous hind legs.

"Come on then, Billy boy, let's get off or we'll be late," said the old man, and, turning to me, said, "I hope the guv'nor'll be all right soon."

"Yes," I thought, "and I hope Billy boy'll be all right."

It was a cold bleak morning in January when I first saw her. Rain was falling in a steady drizzle and she looked a forlorn little figure standing at the crossroads. Dressed in landgirl's uniform: wide-brimmed hat, thick, short, brown overcoat, breeches and stockings, a kit-bag at her feet. Her shoulders were shaking as she waved to some landgirls in the back of a departing lorry. The girls in the lorry were waving and singing;

> "Wish me luck as you wave me goodbye,
> With a smile, not a tear . . ."

The lorry went round a corner and was soon out of sight. The girl at the crossroads continued to stare in the direction which the lorry had taken and did not notice my approach. Not wishing to come upon her unawares I walked more slowly, stepping from the wide grass verge on to the road. The nails of my boots scrunched on the loose chippings of the roadside, the girl turned round and seemed startled to see me. A few tiny tear drops trickled down her face already wet from the rain. She looked so small, helpless and lost.

"Hullo," I said, and added, "It's not a very nice morning, is it?"

"No," she replied, rather hesitantly, "it isn't." She put a hand in her overcoat pocket and pulled out a handkerchief and started dabbing her eyes with a corner of it. I just stood not quite knowing what to say and not quite liking to move away. She smiled, and dimples appeared in her cheeks, and I noticed she had dark brown eyes, although they were still rather wet. She wiped her eyes again, rather vigorously, in rather a businesslike fashion and pushed the handkerchief back in her pocket.

"Can you tell me the way to Mr Clutterbuck's?" she asked, putting a hand down to pick up her bag.

"You're new round here, aren't you? You're not from the hostel near the village?"

"Yes, no," she replied, "I mean, I am new round here and no, I'm not from the hostel near the village."

She had a quiet pleasant voice; and I noticed when she smiled her eyes sparkled and the tears had vanished. "I'll show you the way to Mr Clutterbuck's, I'm going that way," I said, and, suddenly emboldened, "— and I'll carry your bag."

"Oh, that's kind of you," she answered.

I slung the bag over my shoulder and we turned down the road leading to Willow Farm. We walked along in silence for a few moments. I tried hard to think of something to say.

It was the girl who broke the silence. "I'm going to work regularly for Mr Clutterbuck, I shall be living-in at the farmhouse."

I learnt that she'd only recently completed her training and this would be the first time she'd worked on a farm, except in the company of other landgirls.

"I've always lived in a town," she said. "My parents didn't like me joining the Land Army — they thought farm work wasn't the right thing for a girl."

I was glad to be able to tell her that Mr and Mrs Clutterbuck were the kindest of people, and then we lapsed into silence again. The drizzle of rain had increased and now the rain was bouncing on the road. I stole another glance at the girl, noticing her brown hair peeping from under her wide-brimmed hat, the soft

216

curve of her cheek now moist with rain. She perceived my furtive glance and I felt confused. She smiled again, more to herself than to me; I felt more confused, thinking that she was laughing at me. Our roles were reversed. Five minutes ago, she'd been crying and obviously distressed, now she seemed assured and I disconcerted. My confusion turned to a vague sense of irritation, and then Willow Farm came into view.

"There, that's it," I said, pointing with my free hand.

We stopped at the gate which led into the flagged yard in front of the house and I put down her bag.

"Thank you," she said in a small voice, which swept away my irritation, "you've been very kind."

"Oh, that's all right," I replied in what I hoped was an off-hand manner. I gazed down at her feet and mumbled, "I hope you get on all right. I must be getting back to work. Goodbye . . . Miss . . . er . . . er . . . Oh, I don't know your name."

"Molly," she said. "Call me Molly."

"Goodbye, Molly." I walked away. After twenty paces or so, I stopped and turned round. She was just bending down to pick up her bag; seeing me look back, she straightened up and waved.

I didn't see her again for a week or two, and then I saw her on two succeeding nights as I was on my way home. The first night I saw her dimly, just coming out of the barn in the twilight. The next night she was walking across the courtyard and I stopped and spoke to her until I saw Mr Clutterbuck appear, and then I hastily bade her goodnight and jumped on my bicycle.

One evening in the middle of February, I was cycling home. The nights were drawing out and the birds beginning to sing, the roadside banks were flecked with celandine. "Hey!" shouted Mr Clutterbuck as I passed his gate, "Why ain't you taking young Molly to the concert next week?"

"I'd like to," I answered.

"Well then, why don't you? She's a lovely girl."

"I don't like to ask her."

"Well, we'll soon put that right," said Mr Clutterbuck, and shouted, "Molly!"

"Ho, ho, ho," he chuckled, as we heard Molly running towards us. Molly appeared in her dark green pullover. "Yes, Mr Clutterbuck?"

"Molly, why ain't you goin' to the concert with this young man?"

"Because he hasn't asked me, Mr Clutterbuck."

Mr Clutterbuck poked me with his finger and said, "Ask her, lad." Then he gave me a broad wink and said, "Well, I'll go on in and have my tea."

When Molly and I arrived, about ten minutes before the concert was due to start, the schoolroom was already crowded. Molly took off her coat and I saw that she was wearing a brown frock which matched her eyes. We pushed our way to the back of the room and found space to sit on a long wooden form. I was conscious of enquiring eyes as we sat down and was thankful when the oil lamps — the village had no electricity — were turned down low.

The curtains across the stage were closed, a tinkling piano could be heard. The curtains trembled, a hand and then Mr Bence, the vicar, appeared, his long white hair ruffled.

"Good evening, everybody." The pince-nez dropped from his nose and dangled from a cord around his neck. "Once again I welcome you to our annual concert." He drew one curtain back and Mrs Peabody was seen sitting at the piano, very upright and very conscious of being the focus of attention. Mr Bence started to pull the other curtain, but it stuck halfway. Mrs Peabody leapt from the piano stool and strode across to assist him. She tugged at the curtain, Mr Bence tugged and eventually — Mrs Peabody's face getting redder all the while — they managed to draw it aside. "We'll leave the curtains open all the time now," hissed Mr Bence.

Mrs Peabody seated herself primly on the piano stool, smoothed down her skirt and then patted and adjusted her hair. Mr Bence made a flourishing gesture and stepped aside, Mrs Peabody started to play the piano and the concert troupe came tripping on to the stage. At least the front row came tripping; the others did a kind of shuffle on. Among them were Sam Fisher, looking very gawky; tubby Lionel Collins, a smallholder who was always complaining of being worked to death, an opinion held only by himself; Tom Prewett, puffed up like a turkey cock; the Station Master, very solemn; Mr Bingley, whose wraith-like body housed a powerful voice; and, last of all Micah Elford.

The assembled company sang:

"Hello everybody. How do you do,
Hello everybody . . ."

More people had arrived and were still arriving, causing someone to shout, "Shut the doors, mind the blackout." Others squeezed themselves on to the form we were sitting on. Molly was pressed close to me, I felt the warmth of her body against mine, and caught the smell of her perfume.

The opening number concluded, the company marched off. Sam Fisher dropped his cane, which rolled and clattered across the stage. He stopped to pick it up to the mock cheers of a huddle of lads in the audience.

"And now," said Mr Bence, when Sam was out of the way, "and now," he stopped to affix his pince-nez and, peering at a slip of paper, "it is my great pleasure to introduce Miss Isobel Hatch, who is going to sing for us, 'If Winter Comes, With All Its Ice and Snow'."

Isobel was the demure daughter of the formidable Mrs Hatch. Every year she sang the same song. We had more or less the same programme every year, and every year the room was packed. Isobel, her normally pale face flushed, left the stage as the audience applauded; all performers, good or bad, were dutifully applauded. "Bravo, bravo!" shouted Miss Crotcher, in her booming voice.

Mr Bence announced Lionel Collins, who launched into "Seven Years with the Wrong Woman" before Mr Bence had even finished speaking. Mrs Peabody had to miss a few bars in order to catch up with him. As soon as he'd finished and even before Miss Crotcher had finished booming "Bravo," he gave a repeat rendering of the song. He might have gone on to give another, had not Mr Bence forestalled him. With admirable ability he skipped to Lionel's side towards the end of the song and before Lionel could take a deep breath, he cried, "Delightful, Lionel, truly delightful," and ushered him off the stage.

A nudge in my back, and I looked up and saw the vet perched on a cupboard behind me. He must have crept in unnoticed during the performance.

"And now," said Mr Bence, having seen Lionel safely out of the way, "we have a new member of our troupe who is about to perform some conjuring tricks. Ladies and Gentlemen, Mr Micah Elford, Master Magician."

This caused a rustle of surprise, we'd never seen Micah perform before and had no idea he was a conjurer. A little girl carried a baize-topped card table to the centre of the stage, two other little girls placed various apparatus including a top hat, on the table. "Micah, Micah," hissed the Vicar, "come along now, we're all waiting for you." Micah lumbered on stage, almost tripping over a side curtain.

"Bravo, bravo!" boomed Miss Crotcher. Micah stood fumbling with his tie, looking dazed.

"Come on, Micah. Be you gonna do summat or be you just gonna stand there?" shouted Reuben Kimmins.

"Well . . . er . . . um," mumbled Micah in his usual drawling manner. "Well, um, for my first trick — well, er, well . . . I be a bit confused, hang on a minute." Micah drew a slip of paper from his waistcoat pocket and studied it.

"Be you intendin' to produce a stuffed rabbit from that hat, Micah?" shouted Uncle George who was sitting near the stage.

Micah brightened and said, "Ladies and Gentlemen, I am now going to produce a white rabbit from this empty hat." He tipped the hat towards us to show that it was empty.

"You byunt goin' to produce a rabbit from that hat," said Uncle George.

"Ho, yus, I am," replied Micah, triumphantly.

"Ho, no, you byunt," said Uncle George.

"Ho, yus, I am," repeated Micah. Micah was quite perky now. At long last he would be able to score over Uncle George.

"Ho, no, you byunt, you dropped that rabbit when you come round the curtain," said Uncle George.

Poor Micah looked quite crestfallen. Mr Bence crossed the stage, picked up the rabbit and handed it to Micah. "Never mind, Micah," he said kindly. "Go back and come on again."

"No," drawled Micah, "it chun't no good now, that there trick's all spoiled."

"Do the next un then, Micah, old fella," suggested Uncle George.

Molly leaned her head towards mine, her hair brushed the side of my face. "I know that man," she whispered. "He's often at the farm. I call him Uncle George."

"He is my Uncle George," I whispered back.

"I think he's sweet," said Molly. "But he was a bit unkind to the conjurer."

222

Micah did a few tricks, but he never recovered from the shock of losing the rabbit and most of his performance was poor. But we all applauded heartily and Miss Crotcher boomed "bravo" even louder.

We had two more singing acts. Mrs Ellicot from the Rose and Crown, wearing a large feathered hat and a long feather boa and carrying a stuffed parrot in a cage, sang "My Old Man, said Follow the Van" and the Station Master, who had a good bass voice sang, "Red Sails in the Sunset".

A loud knocking on the door created a diversion. Mr Cordwell burst in and shouted, "Is the vet here, is the vet here? I've got a cow calving, she's in a bad way."

"Coming, Mr Cordwell," said the vet, and clambered down from the cupboard.

"Ah," said a relieved Mr Cordwell. "They told me I'd find you here. Me and the boys couldn't manage and there ain't no time to lose."

"Come on, then," cried the vet, already at the door.

"I'll come and give you a hand," said Fred Jenkins, himself a cowman. The three of them left and the Station Master finished his song.

Two girls, evacuees living with Mr Pontifex, did a tap dance. Their performance was accomplished — Mr Pontifex's housekeeper, Gert, had been an actress and she had, no doubt, coached them. The girls, flushed with pleasure from the loud applause, curtsied and left the stage.

A girl of seventeen or eighteen, who'd only recently come to live in the village, also danced. Hers was a polished performance. Mrs Peabody's playing did not do it justice. She wore a very short skirt and when she kicked her long legs into the air, brief, frilly knickers were exposed. A group of lads in the corner whistled. Though Miss Crotcher boomed her usual bravo, at the conclusion of her dancing, the applause was sparse and several women looked shocked and muttered, "Well, I never!" and, "If I were her mother, I know what I'd do."

"Now, we have a veteran trouper," said Mr Bence, after we'd had a long monologue from Mr Bingley, "Mr Sam Fisher is about to sing two of his comic songs for you."

Sam shuffled on stage, all arms and legs and waggling moustache. He wore a top hat and carried pigskin gloves and a silver-topped ebony cane. "Good evening," said Sam, and shook his head. In an aside to the Vicar, he said, "Three, Vicar, three. Hup, hup, hup," cried Sam and pranced across the stage, waving his cane. He turned, and crying "Hup, hup, hup," pranced over to Mrs Peabody at the piano. "Right, Mrs P.," he cried with an attempt at gaiety, "let it rip.

"I'm Burlington Bertie," sang Sam, in a doleful voice, a bit off-key. Then he sang, "I'm Gilbert, the Filbert". Flip-flop went his arms and legs as he sang, and he waggled his head and occasionally banged the cane on the stage.

"Isn't he awful," whispered Molly.

"Yes," I answered, "he is. He's my uncle too."

"Oh, I'm sorry," said Molly.

"You needn't be. We all know how awful he is, except Aunt Aggie, that's his wife." I could see Aunt Aggie, a proud expression on her face.

"Is your father here?" asked Molly.

"No. He never comes to village concerts."

"Your mother?"

"No. She couldn't come." I didn't tell her that Mother had refused because she said she wasn't going to be humiliated by Sam Fisher, or Uncle George.

"Now, here's a rouser for yer," said Uncle Sam, and sang "Knocked 'em in the Old Kent Road". But it wasn't very rousing, not the way Sam sang it.

"D'you want another, Vicar?" asked Sam, as Mr Bence stepped forward. "Just one more real old rib tickler?"

"It's very kind of you, Mr Fisher, but really you've been more than generous with us tonight," said Mr Bence, and the lads in the corner groaned.

"I could manage one more, Vicar, a rare old rollicker."

"No, Mr Fisher, you must be very tired after all your effort."

"I be tired, Vicar, but I could have done it."

"Extremely kind, extremely kind, but I wouldn't hear of it," said Mr Bence, gently propelling him off the stage.

"Phew, what a nasty smell," I heard Mrs Hatch say.

"Ah, it's Len Wilson's filthy old wellingtons," said Uncle George, loudly. "They'm smot up with cow muck and stale milk, an' now it's got warm in here they've started to pong."

Tom Prewett, wearing a straw hat, white trousers — far too short — and an old faded cricket blazer was now on stage telling jokes. Some of his jokes were rather coarse and at the side of the stage, I could see the Vicar

225

frowning. "Not quite the thing," I heard Mrs Gosworth remark. A few more turns and then the Vicar said, "And now we come to our finale."

"We want George to sing 'Farmer's Boy'," cried Reuben.

"Yes, yes," shouted the others, including Colonel. "We want George to sing 'Farmer's Boy'."

"He allus do," said Reuben.

Uncle George stood up. "Right-ho."

"Come on, George," said Mr Bence, smiling and extending a hand to help him on to the stage.

"Do you remember the tune, Missus?" Uncle George asked Mrs Peabody. Mrs Peabody glared at him and started playing.

"The sun had set beyond yon hill
Across a dreary moor,"

sang Uncle George in a deep baritone.

"When weary and lame,
A boy there came up to a farmer's door,"

When he reached the chorus everyone joined in,

"To plough and to sow,
To reap and to mow
And to be a farmer's boy,
To be a farmer's boy."

After the performance we met Aunt Aggie. "Wasn't Sam good tonight," she said. "Oh, didn't I laugh. I was so proud of him. But I expect the poor old fellow's bathered right out, he puts so much go into it."

Aunt Aggie was staring at Molly. "Is this your young lady?" she asked. I introduced them. Aunt Aggie lowered her voice and said in a confidential manner, "Are you a flirt, my dear?" And, fortunately, without waiting for an answer, she said, "I was a dreadful flirt, he, he, he." Aunt Aggie suddenly looked very serious — "until I met Sam. Oh, he was so handsome in those days. Turned my heart right over, he did."

Uncle George joined us. "Well, well, well," he rumbled, his eyes atwinkle, "I'm glad you two young people know one another."

"Hello, Uncle George," said Molly.

"You know this young lady, George?" asked Aunt Aggie.

"Of course I do. We're old friends, ain't we, Molly?"

"I was just telling her what a flirt I was when I was her age," said Aunt Aggie. "You remember what a flirt I was, don't you, George?"

"Ah, I seem to recall summat of the sort," said Uncle George in a rather uninterested way. He turned to face Molly and me. "You two young people must come and have tea with me one Sunday. Aggie'll make some cake, won't you, Aggie?"

"Oh yes," said Aunt Aggie. "And you'll have to come and visit Sam and me one evening." She paused and looked thoughtful before saying, "Does your mother know this young lady?"

"Time to be goin' home," said Uncle George.

"Wasn't Sam good tonight, George," she said, her usually mournful face showing some animation.

"First class, absolutely first class," said Uncle George, turning to give Molly and me a wink. "First class, Aggie. I think you'd better get him home now, after all the gusto he put in that singing he'll be tired right out."

"Yes, I must get him home and make him comfy." Aunt Aggie looked very woeful. "My poor old Sam's not very well you know. It's the strain of that factory, all the shifty work and metal fatigue," she said to Molly.

"Goodnight, Aggie," said Uncle George.

"Goodnight." Aunt Aggie walked away, stopped, turned round and said, "When you bring the young lady to see us, perhaps, if he's not too tired, Sam will sing another of his comic songs."

"Ah, that'll be very nice for them," said Uncle George.

CHAPTER
ELEVEN

A hard winter

Last year when we started hoeing the roots the war in Europe had just ended. "You just mark my words, Jack," Mr Saggamore had said, chopping with increased vigour, as if to give emphasis to his words, "they'll flood this country with imported food now." But here we were in May 1946 and food was as scarce as it had been at any time during the war. Labour was even scarcer; the Italian prisoners of war had returned to Italy. Big Willy was still with us, but he too would soon be leaving.

Caleb, who had become very doddery, had retired. Most days he could be seen, still clad in breeches leggings and heavy boots, leaning over his garden gate, waiting to waylay someone with whom he could talk over "the good old days", when things were done properly, and prophesy the return of the horses some day.

Old Mr Williams, now rather feeble, still visited the harvest fields most days, and talked of harvests and horses of long ago. It was a wet time during harvest and we were late finishing. After harvest Big Willy left us; soon he would be back on that little farm in Germany and reunited with his wife and daughters.

Mr Saggamore tried to coax local men, those returned from the forces and now working in factories, to help us in the evenings and at weekends, with the hay, the corn or the root harvest, but found few takers. And those who came, came but once or twice and then avoided us or made excuses.

"They won't have it," said Mr Ford one day, when he'd dismounted from his bicycle and found a convenient place to sit. Mr Ford was a big man — it was a marvel that old bicycle of his withstood his great bulk, no wonder it had two cross-bars — and getting on in years. He was an agent for a firm of fertiliser manufacturers, specialising in basic slag. He also sold cattle medicines and sundry household goods — mainly polish, tins of which were usually strapped to the carrier on the back of his bicycle.

He was regarded as a bit of a nuisance in the district; he was persistent — especially about the polish. When he came he stopped, perhaps hoping he would be given an order, even if it were only to get rid of him. Not that he talked much, in fact he spoke very slowly and sparsely, but there was a heaviness about him. He seemed able to create a depressing atmosphere. He was also able to immobilise his victim, forcing the unfortunate person to suffer the whole of his dreary performance.

"Polish," he would grunt and breath heavily. A long pause and then in sepulchral tone, "Do you want any polish?" By now he would be sitting down — he always found somewhere to sit — and be doing some heavy breathing in earnest, his eyes drooping and showing the red of the inner bottom lids. "You must want some polish or something," he would say gloomily. If he saw a pig, a cat or a dog: "That animal don't look none too well. I should say he's going to die very soon." This comment would be made a little more cheerfully. A long silence would ensue — Mr Ford had some knack which almost rendered his listeners dumb. At this stage he would take a pinch of snuff and then stare morosely into space. "I've got some stuff on my bike though that would put him right."

Mr Ford was an inveterate scrounger, eggs, apples, cider, pigmeat — he seemed to have a sixth sense about pig-killing — anything. And in the autumn, much to farmers' annoyance, he would often abandon his selling to pick mushrooms from their fields. Ironically, the slag Ford sold killed mushrooms.

But most farmers tolerated him, partly because he was a local man, but mainly because they were glad to obtain the slag which was in short supply. The basic slag — basic usually pronounced bassic — was a by-product of the steel industry: a fine black powder, rich in phosphate and invaluable on our heavy land.

"No," said Mr Ford, on that day in late September, when he finally decided to go, "they won't have it today, you won't get chaps to work on the land any more."

"No," said Mr Saggamore, when Ford was out of earshot, "chaps won't have farmwork now. And that fat old chap never would have work neither, never done a day's work in his life. I wonder the firm still let him have the agency. But we're lucky to get that slag, it pays to humour the old varmint."

It was a blustery day in November when Jack and I went to the station to fetch the slag. Mrs Tunney was in her shed, busy shelling chestnuts. She stopped to roll a cigarette while she told us the slag was in the end railway truck. "I'd come down with you, kid," she said, thrusting the end of her cigarette in the fire to light it, "but I'm pretty damned busy at the moment."

The slag was in an open truck covered with a stiff tarpaulin which had caved in and collected the rain, so that we were faced with something like a miniature swimming pool. We baled the water out with some station buckets and removed the heavy tarpaulin and saw a mess of slag. The bags of slag must have been tipped into the truck and were wedged together. Some of the bags were wet, some were burst open. Some of the slag had set hard as concrete, some of it whirled — a fine black dust — around the truck. It covered our hands, stuck to our faces, and got into our eyes.

"Huh," remarked Jack, "we're very lucky to get it." Mr Ford came along on his bicycle. "He don't half bear down on that poor old bike," said Jack.

"Hullo, Ford, you old flirt," we heard Mrs Tunney shout.

Ford ignored her and rode purposefully on towards us. "You are lucky to have that," he grunted.

"So we've bin told," said Jack.

Ford had propped his bicycle against a truck and found a box to sit on. "Want anything in the household line, Musgrove?" he asked.

"Ah, some free soap to wash this slag off with," replied Jack.

Ford took a pinch of snuff and stared into space.

"It weren't half in a pickle, just dumped in here. Bags bust, a lot of the slag was loose an' we've had to shut it into other bags or shovel it up," said Jack.

Ford just stared morosely into space, grunting. "It's goin' to be a damned hard winter," he said at last, and mounted his bicycle and rode away.

Ford was right. It was the damnedest, hardest, cruellest winter within living memory. And to make matters worse, food and fuel were desperately short. Jack and I were hedge-laying in a distant field on the morning the snow started to fall. The ground was hard and dry and frozen, the snow remained where it fell. At dinner time we pushed our tools under the hedge ready for our return in the afternoon. At two o'clock the snow was several inches deep and falling hard. It was months before we returned.

It snowed all night, deep crisp stuff, over a foot deep in the fields and it drifted into our sunken lanes and blocked them. Several days that winter I had to walk to and from work. We had to dig a roadway to the main road and take the churns of milk there by horse and cart. But more snow fell and drifted into the lanes, blocking them again. Farms and houses were cut off; delivery vans and lorries were unable to reach us. Everyone went about on foot, occasionally by horse and cart, or slithered on bicycles when pathways were cleared. We were isolated, thrown back on our own resources. Sometimes the only way to walk was on top of the hedges blocked tight with snow. The deep lane leading to Suttridge remained blocked for weeks; we dug a roadway across the fields for the milk cart. We milked the cows and tended the stock, but all other farm work stopped.

And yet, despite the bitter cold and the hardship, I enjoyed it. To see the world clothed in a white mantle of innocence each day, the hushed atmosphere, and everyone so friendly, "No enemy but winter and rough weather" — and shortages of nearly everything. Even to arrive at work was an achievement. On bright, sunny days, when there wasn't any wind, the snow reflected the heat and it was quite warm. But as the vivid red sun slowly sank behind the Forest hills, the day grew crisply chill. On such days, Jack would remark with grim foreboding, "The brighter the day, the sharper the night."

The ice on the drinking ponds became thicker and iron bars were needed to break it. The water began to freeze over even as we broke the ice; and the water receded, so that it was necessary to make a hole a little further in each day. Mangolds froze solid in clamps, no matter how thickly covered with straw and hedge trimmings. The War Ag's huge store of potatoes, it was reputed, was ruined. Sheep were buried alive in snowdrifts, and out-wintered cattle huddled under the hedges with icicles dangling from their shaggy coats.

Starvation made wild life increasingly bold. The single file footprints of the fox could be seen in the snow around houses, barns and sheds. Pheasants would visit the yards, even in daylight; the wood pigeons stripped the ivy berries and would come within a foot or two of us as we worked; and rabbits gnawed at the bark at the toughest of old apple trees.

234

On these cold mornings it was pleasant to start the day's work by milking the cows which were housed in the shed, warm from the heat of their bodies. Mr Saggamore stuffed old sacks under the doorways to keep out the draught. Pleasant, thrusting your head into the warm flank of a cow as you sat on a stool milking her. The light from the hurricane lanterns slung from the rafters gave the shed a rosy glow. Yes, it was cosy in there, hearing the milk pinging into the bottom of the bucket between your knees. As the bucket began to fill the sound changed from "ping-ping" to "fuzz-fuzz". And looking out from the tiny windows to see the dawn breaking and the grey sky. The snow, and the icicles hanging outside and the sound of the howling wind, only gave enchantment to the shed inside. The steady munching of the cows, the rustling of straw underfoot, and the jangle of the chains round the cows' necks. The smell of the cows, the milk, the aroma of roots and hay. And in late afternoon as we milked again, seeing the daylight fade and the glistening snow on the rooftops.

Pleasant indeed, unless a cow kicked and knocked the milk over you. That could be very unpleasant, especially on a cold morning. First you were warm with milk and then cold, and when your clothes dried you were left with the cloying stink of stale milk. And if the cow really lashed out, you toppled or were thrown from the stool into the gutter to be bruised and covered with dung.

It didn't happen often, but occasionally was quite enough. A few of the cows were fidgety and you had to be on your guard. Two or three were bad tempered and your right hand had to be continually alert, ready to grab the bucket. One cow — Buttercup — was usually quiet, but once in a while she would kick viciously and quickly; too suddenly for the milker to forestall her or to grab the bucket.

"Oho," Jack would calmly say when it happened to someone else, "old Buttercup 'ave got it on 'er." But he wasn't so calm when he was the one who ignobly landed in the gutter and arose dripping with milk.

We were into March when Mr Tucker, the butcher, came to cut up the bacon pig at Suttridge. The snow had lessened. He came just as we had finished milking, and, as he arrived, stamping his feet — he had walked — it started to snow again, heavier than it had before. By the time he'd finished the snow lay several feet deep, and was piled up by doors and walls. "I've been going to bed with a shovel for weeks," he remarked. We trudged back to the village together, snow still falling thickly.

The snow and the frost lasted from 21 January until 14 March, and afterwards came floods and the gales. Uncle George pronounced it "a master of a winter", and even the oldest habitué of the Lion (where, incidentally, the beer had frozen), admitted he "had never seen the like on't, never in all his born days".

Mr Clutterbuck quoted the old music hall song:

"We've been together now for forty years,
An' it don't seem a day too much."

The occasion was Mr and Mrs Clutterbuck's fortieth wedding anniversary. They were giving a little party to celebrate the event. Molly was present; many of the landgirls had left the district, but Molly remained, she was part of the Clutterbuck family now, as it were.

Ever since that concert last year, Molly and I had been meeting regularly — well, fairly regularly.

Mr Clutterbuck handed round glasses of sherry, the celebration cake was cut. Mr Clutterbuck made a short speech, displaying a quiet sense of humour. Looking at Mrs Clutterbuck, her white hair, her placid face, her frail, genteel body, it was difficult to realise the years of arduous work she'd done. The large house, the poultry, the hours spent turning the butter churn — yes, it was difficult to believe now, until you looked at her hands — knotted and work-worn. I'd learnt to look at people's hands.

A few words from a friend or two, you'd hardly call them speeches, just a few words in token of the occasion. More sherry, and the party split into two, male and female. The females spoke of their children, grandchildren. The men talked of farming, as farmers always do when they're gathered together.

Mr Clutterbuck said he could "see the writing on the wall" for farming, its days of prosperity numbered.

"Surely not," said one; "the new Agricultural Act," put in another. Mr Clutterbuck shook his head, "I've seen it all before. They passed the Corn Production Act after the 'fourteen war and then repealed it, and they'll repeal this new Act when it suits 'em. No, I've been caught once, this time I'll get out while the going's good."

"Do you mean you're going to retire?" we exclaimed.

At the word "retire" equal the party grew together again. "Do you mean you're going to retire, Father?" asked Mr Clutterbuck's daughter. Her face brightened, "It'll make life so much easier for Mother, this great house." And then her face clouded, "But, Father, whatever will you do? You'll be lost without a farm."

"I'm looking out for a little place with half a dozen acres, where I can keep a few cattle," her father told her. "And then I can still pretend I'm a farmer."

Coffee and sandwiches were brought into the sitting room, the party shuffled round. Later, when conversation had become desultory, I looked across the room and saw Mr and Mrs Clutterbuck sitting side by side. Despite all their troubles, there they were, still side by side, after forty years, still happy together. I glanced across at Molly, our eyes met; and I knew that Molly was the only girl for me.

ISIS publish a wide range of books in large print, from fiction to biography. A full list of titles is available free of charge from the address below. Alternatively, contact your local library for details of their collection of ISIS large print books.

Details of ISIS complete and unabridged audio books are also available.

Any suggestions for books you would like to see in large print or audio are always welcome.

ISIS

7 Centremead
Osney Mead
Oxford OX2 0ES
(01865) 250333